ANDY LO RUSSO

Sing & Cook Italian

December 12, 2002.
To Leslie & Tom + Tomezee
Buon Natale
Andy Lo Russo

Happy Heart Publishing

SANTA BARBARA • 1993

ISBN No. 0-9622020-1-0

10 9 8 7 6 5 4 3 2 1

Published by Happy Heart Publishing
Post Office Box 91725, Santa Barbara, California 93190-1725.

Design and Typography: Jim Cook
Cover Design: Tom Leja
Photos: John Sirois
Cover Support Group: Beda Marc, Leslie Brice, John Sirois
The publisher wishes to thank Santa Barbara Stone and Jordanos Market for use of
    material on the cover
Environmental Design: Nena Spencer
Nutritional Consultant: Patricia Wood
Family Recipes: Grandmother Grace, Aunt Rose, Aunt Janet, Momma Lo Russo,
    Cousins John & Maria Frey

Italian Lyric Coach: Carla Reineri
Voic Constructionist: Giovanna d'Onofrio
Audiotape recorded at Gateway Studio, Carpinteria, California
Conductor/Piano: Donald Carl Eugster
Engineer, Jeff Peters
Musicians: Joseppi Scozzaro (accordion), Tom Marion (guitar and mandoline), Paul
    Shelasky (violin/guitar), Kitten Tanner (bass, cello), Sara Schwartz (flute)
Source for biographies: Grove Dictionary of Music

The author wishes to thank Ida Lo Russo, Ron Lo Russo, Nena Spencer, Cassandra
Harris, Barbara Greene, Rosanne Coit, Lexi Kern, and Giovanna d'Onofrio for their
support.

Contents

The Family (ca. 1950)

Food from the Land of Song

IN ITALY EVERYBODY SINGS! From the people on the street and the workers in the fields to the city dwellers and businesspeople, everybody sings. That's why it's called the "land of song."

Italy's is a rich culture, filled with music and song. Everywhere one looks, one finds a work of art. Italians themselves are a work of art, and this is exemplified especially in their food.

The neighborhood in which I grew up was like that. We would sing on the street corners and in the tunnels around the city. We would sing *a cappella* (unaccompanied) and people would gather around and sometimes join in. There was always a *pizzeria* close by, and the smell of fresh garlic and tomatoes would stir our taste buds and inspire us to sing more.

Sometimes, one of the boys would want to impress a girl, and our group of singers would gather outside her house, under her window, and sing love songs. The girl being serenaded would eventually stick her head out the window and throw a kiss to us—but not before her father would tells us to move on or he would call the police!

We sang at all the family picnics and the weddings. My uncle's band would play the standard Italian songs and we, not always understanding the words, would sing along, having a great time anyway. I remember the weddings as being like those in *The Godfather*—everyone would dance and sing for as long as the band played.

In the fifth grade I was asked to get up in front of the class and sing one of the popular songs, "Teenager in Love." I felt shy standing there, so I put on my best smile and pretended to be on a street corner. I did so well that they asked me to sing again on the bus during a field trip. I never forgot the experience. I've always won people over with a song whenever I got the chance.

Singing opens up a whole new world. Try it. It doesn't matter what anyone says or thinks, just do it. Whatever comes out is divine. The more you sing, the more confidence you achieve and, before you know it, you'll be right up there on stage with the best of them.

Food: The Gift of Love

Growing up in an Italian neighborhood in New Jersey was like living in Italy. The Italian food market on the way to school always had some magical, alluring aroma emanating from its doors. I would be drawn into its spell and, once inside, be filled with the smells of fresh parmesan and romano cheese balls hanging in the window. The sight of fresh mozzarella cheese (and I mean the kind where the milk is oozing out of it and not the rubbery kind that you find in the supermarket) was enough to make my mouth water. This is not to mention the rows of fresh-made pasta and the barrels of olives. The sausage was made fresh every day and would hang in the case where the pastas were.

The bread was fresh from the Italian bakery down the street, and that alone would make one want to stop and buy everything in the store. I remember that bakery on the way to church or school. Every morning it was filled with people buying up everything in the store. One had to get there early for some breads. I always ate the ends before I got home. They were delicious!

I grew up on 100-percent Italian food. My mother, a first-generation Italian-American, learned to cook from her mother, Grace, who was born in Agira in eastern Sicily. My father, also first generation, learned to cook from his mother, who was born in southern Italy, the region of Lucania-Potenza. I loved to listen to my grandfather's stories of when he was a young boy. His family had a farm on which they raised goats and chickens—fresh eggs, cheese, and milk every day. Their vegetables came right out of their garden.

Hard work, family, and lots of time together: It was a simple life with simple pleasures. My Grandmother Grace would listen to the operas every chance she had. I was exposed to the great singers as my grandmother listened to the great music while cooking. The music, the voices, the orchestras are ingrained in my bones forever.

There is a definite link between food and family in Italy. Food shared at the table is a gift of love, a way of showing others how much one cares for them and their health. I feel that this is one of the reasons that the family group remains so strong with Italians. There isn't a day that goes by that Italians don't talk about food. We talk about the next meal while we're eating the one before us. Food is an Italian's way of giving love from the heart.

There are many different types of cooking in Italy. Each region has its own specialties and methods of preparation. Northern, central, and southern Italy had broken into twenty-three regions, each with its own culture, dialect, and food. *Mangia* ("to eat") is a magic word; I learned it from Grandmother Grace, who was always ready to open the refrigerator and cook a meal for anyone who walked into her kitchen. "*Dio ti benedici* (God bless you)," she would say, and start cooking.

A Festival in the Kitchen

My aspiration has always been to be a well-known international singing sensation. Now that I've tapped into my ethnic roots, it's songs and culture, La Scala seems closer at hand. What would it be like to walk up on stage at the Met or La Scala and sing the beautiful Italian arias from my ancestors? Whenever I sing, whether a local town concert or in my kitchen, I put as much into it as if I were there on stage in those world famous concert halls.

I love going to ethnic festivals, and especially entertaining at them. Food, song, and dance seem to go together very well. I find myself transported to whatever country is being fêted—France, Spain, Greece, Italy. It becomes a trip around the world.

Cooking, too, is like a festival in one's own kitchen. Invite all your family and friends and have them sing and cook with you. The food, you'll find, tastes better. We need to get back to where we all eat together more often. It's hard in this era of two-family income earners, when we're all running helter-skelter and eating on the run, to enjoy a home-cooked meal. Our fixation on fast-food is not good for our digestion. We need to slow down, set apart some time each week to get together with family and friends and sing and cook a great meal.

. . .

This cookbook was a long time coming. After all, I can go to only so many friends' houses and cook and sing before I run out friends (which

I never seem to do). There's always someone inviting me over to cook and sing for them. I've been asked for my recipes for so long that I decided to put them into a book and send them out to the universe.

Eating is a spiritual experience, and the food we eat becomes us. (Sound familiar?) One of the most important things in the preparation of good food, as well as eating it, is one's frame of mind. It's essential to be relaxed in both mind and body, and that's where singing helps. A good frame of mind lets us enjoy our food and digest it better, getting the maximum nutrition from it. Good conversation, a relaxed environment, and joyful thoughts all lend to a great meal. Smells are important. Just smelling your food, the digestive process starts immediately.

It's important to use only fresh ingredients, spices, and seasonings in your cooking. A simple life—eat, sing, and be happy.

. . .

This book is written to help us get the most out of life in each moment. It is dedicated to all those lovers of *romanza*, good food, and good times . . . to my family, aunts, uncles, cousins, and friends who have shared their love with me at the dinner table and get-togethers all over the country: *Lasciamo che la morte ci trovi pieni di vita!* (Let death find us filled with life!)

I would like this book, with its songs and recipes, to bring a little bit of fun and celebration to all who use it. I am grateful to all my teachers, friends, lovers, and guardian angels who have traveled with me this far, and all those who are yet to come.

Music: Our Sweetest Joy

"SONG IS MAN'S SWEETEST JOY," said the bard Musaeus, and Atheneauis reported in the second century that "it is no disgrace to confess that one knows nothing, but it is deemed a disgrace to decline to sing."

"Pure and bright as the sound of silver," said someone back in the sixteenth century who had just heard a *castrato* sing. Since much of the music at the time was written in the soprano range, and as women were not allowed in the church choirs, young boys with particularly beautiful voices would be castrated so that their voices wouldn't change at puberty. It was a popular way to give a man the soprano voice. I am, however, glad that the custom is no longer practiced.

The seventeen and eighteenth centuries are characterized by several musical trends: the rise of the professional opera star, the wide popularity of the *castrato*, the development of the Italian-style of singing known as *bel canto* (beautiful singing), and the cultivation of vocal ornamentation and artifice.

My Daily Singing Preparation

I enjoy going for a long bike ride into the mountains around Ojai, California, where I live. Each morning I take an eight-mile journey up one of the many mountain paths that overlook the beautiful valley. I put my bike into an easy peddle gear and pump up the winding trails that snake around the orchards of orange and avocados. Orange blossoms are one of the world's most intoxicating smells.

I bike to a special place, a p*iazza* at the top of a mountain, take out my pitch pipe, and sing my voice scales from low to high C. As I look over the valley I'm transported to sunny Italy or Greece. The crystal-clear blue sky and the golden glow of the sun burning off the fog below lends its own magic. This is when the beautiful Italian melodies come to

11

me. As I hear myself sing, it seems my voice is coming through me, not from me. Each note, as clear as a bell, resonates and fills the valley with song. The smells of sage, lavender, and eucalyptus start my digestive juices flowing, and the magic starts to happen.

Music touches our emotions as no other form of communication can. Our inner emotional life is reflected in our physical surroundings, and singing can play an important and active part in creating whatever reality we desire in our lives. Like everyone, I want to fill my life with feelings of love and happiness, so I listen to and sing songs that feed those positive emotions in my life. When I sing, especially in Italian, I tap into those deep places in my heart that move my emotions and enable me to feel and experience the life force flowing through me, the feeling of being alive in that moment.

I've tapped into my ancestry deep in my DNA. When I sing Italian songs, there is something special and magical. I'm not just a singer singing songs. I become the song, and the emotion and passion flows through me. Sing the scale below everyday.

E E E E Ah Ah Ah Ah Ah Ah Ah Oh Oh Oh Ooh

"Each note has the right to live."
—ARTURO TOSCANNINI

12

Real Magic

"What you are for empowers you.
What you are against weakens you."
(DR. WAYNE DYER)

In my life now, as I notice and observe the workings of the everyday thoughts and desires that fill my mind, I find one thing is certain: Nothing in this physical world ever remains the same. Everything is constantly changing. One must allow oneself to achieve a state of non-change each day to enable that creative energy to flow through one in the most effective way. It helps one grow and helps center the mind. It gives some depth to each and every day. It works for me.

My days start out with my meditation program, consisting of yoga asanas, prana yama (breathing technique), and a morning warm-sesame oil self-massage. I sit quietly and practice a very ancient technique of meditation that allows me to tap into that place of non-change within myself. My best songs and recipes come to me at this time.

It doesn't matter what one has done in the past. The past doesn't equal the future, it is said. What's important is being alive every moment. That's one of the reasons I've decided to make no compromises with my happiness and well being. We have the choice to manifest whatever we put our attention on. The more we serve from the place of true giving and caring for the world, the more we get back from it. It's a simple law of nature. Living life simply, with integrity and truthfulness, is all one can do to allow life to flow with little effort, like the river to the ocean.

Preparing for the Italian Dinner

IT WASN'T HARD TO PUT THIS BOOK TOGETHER. The subject, singing and cooking (especially Italian), is close to my heart. I've met few people who would turn down a great Italian dinner, no matter what the season. And I've met few people who would object to a love song or two before, during, or after a meal.

When I sing while cooking, I'm put in a particular state of mind, like traveling in Italy . . . floating down the river in a gondola with someone special, or high on a mountain overlooking the azure-blue Mediterranean. The beautiful Italian melodies conjure up visions of an accordion, a sweet violin, or a grand piano that go tenderly and directly to my heart—and into the food I'm preparing.

When considering which recipes to include, I went right to the storehouse of the family jewels: my family, my aunts, and, of course, Mama Lo Russo. My Grandmother Grace cooked with a pinch of this, and a shake of that. When she was growing up, there was no refrigeration, so everything was prepared fresh, right from the garden. The pasta was made by hand with fresh ingredients and put into the sun to dry. Vegetables were picked just before being used, and the sauces cooked for hours.

Some of the these recipes call for meat, but I've picked ones that I would cook for my friends and myself. I've sometimes substituted egg white for the whole egg, and reduced the amount of salt, which reflects my own lifestyle and makes the food accessible to those who won't eat Italian foot because of the "fat and cholesterol." A star (*) is next to my favorite recipes. *Buon appetite!*

Eating Italian the Weight-conscious Way

It's important to clear up the myth of the Italian diet. Many people associate Italian cuisine with over-indulgence and see themselves only gaining weight. Italian food is "indulgent" because it's delicious, with lush textures and flavors, but its reputation for putting on pounds is undeserved.

The nutritional foundation of Italian food is pasta, a complex carbohydrate. It takes longer to digest than the simple carbohydrates, such as sugar. Pasta's benefits are twofold: (1) your body receives the energy-giving sugar at a steady rate, avoiding the crash-and-burn blood-sugar cycle of simple carbohydrates, and (2) you stay sated for a longer time. This is good for those physically active people who need lots of reserve fuel.

What one puts on the pasta, however, is what can put on the weight. If you're weight conscious, look for light, oil-based sauces that are tossed with herbs, seafood or vegetables, and fresh, garden tomatoes. Olive oil is a great nutritional plus—this mono-unsaturated fat is credited with helping lower the cholesterol level in the blood.

A word about pizza. Italian connoisseurs watching their waistlines can enjoy pizza. It's an excellent opportunity for a nutritional meal. It helps to choose the ingredients carefully. Whole-wheat and whole-grain crust and low-fat or skim-milk mozzarella is a plus, as are vegetables like peppers, mushrooms, broccoli, artichoke hearts, and—my favorite—olives and sun-dried tomatoes. Yes, you can enjoy pizza without guilt.

The Italian Dinner

The dinner table at my house was always a time of great joy, especially around the holidays like Christmas. Grandmother Grace and all her children would help her prepare a twelve-course feast, everything from soup to nuts. The dinner would start with different types of fish (Sicily is a great seaport), influenced by the "catch of the day." *Baccala,* dried and breaded; *calamari* (squid) stuffed with crab or lobster; raw shrimp in a garlic butter sauce; mussels in *marinara;* crabs in season served in *marinara* with *capillini* (angel hair) pasta. One of my favorite holiday dishes was *Pasta Mudica,* a long tube-type pasta served with sardines, olive oil, and seasoned bread crumbs. Always there would be parmesan and romano cheeses and, of course, fresh bread.

Then came the pastas: *gnocci,* a type of dumpling served with vegetables, *cavatelli* and fresh broccoli, clams and linguine, raviolis with *marinara* and, sometimes, *lasagna* with lots of mozzarella cheese.

The dessert trays were filled with the most colorful assortment of cookies and pastries you could imagine. *Cannolis, sfogliatelle,* chocolate rum-balls rolled in chocolate jimmys, and the famous "S" cookies, dipped in honey or filled with almond paste. Most of these recipes are in this book, but some have been lost over the years.

The Shopping List

TOOLS
Pasta pot (2-6 gallon, sometimes with a colander included)
Wooden spoons
Food processor
Salad spinner
Sharp knives and a good cutting board
Garlic masher
Cheese grater
Measuring cups and spoons
Dishes (hand-painted Italian, if available)
Pasta servers (salad tongs or pasta claws)
Table cloth (colorful)

SPICES
Garlic, oregano, basil, black and white pepper, rosemary, parsley, bay leaves, nutmeg, crushed red pepper, marjoram, sage, thyme.

FOODS
Pasta (imported, all shapes and sizes)
Olives (green, black, and kalamata [Greek])
Cheeses (parmesan, romano, and fresh mozzarella)
Butter
Olive oil (virgin; it's less expensive by the gallon)
Tomatoes (sun-dried, fresh, or canned: whole, purée, stewed, crushed, or paste when fresh isn't available)
Vegetables (artichoke hearts, lettuce, broccoli, spinach, mushrooms)
Italian bread (fresh!)
Pine nuts (*pinoltas*)

Almond paste
Vinegar (balsemic, white, and red-wine with garlic)
Anchovies and sardines
Capers
Coffee
Risotto (rice, the Arborio type)

FOR DESSERT—LA DOLCE VITA
Rum extract
Anise or anisette
Nuts (slivered almonds, hazelnuts, brazil nuts, pine nuts, chopped
    walnuts)
Baking powder
Cocoa (chocolate shavings)
Nutmeg
Eggs (optional)
Vanilla and almond extracts
Espresso coffee
Champagne biscuits
Whipping cream (fresh)
Sugar (confectioner's and white)

The Romantic Evening Kit

Candles—any type, shape, or size that will help set the mood.
Any Pavarroti CD (I like his greatest hits) or tape by Andy Lo Russo
    (okay! Caruso and Domingo will do just fine). Have them ready to
    go into the sound system.
Fresh flowers of any kind, everywhere, especially roses in season.
Fresh herbs—I keep fresh basil, peppermint, oregano, and garlic close
    by. It's amazing how the smell of these will get anyone's digestion
    going.
Beverages—there are many good brands of non-alcoholic wines and
    champagnes available if you don't prefer the real thing.
Someone special to share the experience with.

Some Thoughts on Food

VINO (Wine)
I always felt the earth move after having a few sips of my grandfather Lo Russo's "dago red" wine. I guess it must have been one of the reasons he lived to be over eighty-five years old. There are many Italian varietal wines available in the U.S., among them Chianti, Valpocello, Brunello, Primativo, Nebbiolo, and Spumante.

OLIVE OIL
The quality of the olive oil, they say, depends not on the quality of the olive, but in the way it is processed. The lighter the color, the more refined it is and the more flavor it has. Pure olive oil is great for salads, fine olive oil is excellent for frying. Extra virgin is best for salads—it is full of

---

Pronouncing Italian

VOWELS	*Sound*	*As in . . .*
a	ah	yacht
ĕ	eh	net
e	ay	hay
i	ee	feet
o	oh	rope
u	oo	cool
CONSONANTS		
ci	chee	cheese
ce	chay	chafe
ca	kah	cadenza
cu	koh	cuckoo
che	kay	okay
chi	key	key
gi	jee	jeans
ge	jay	jay
gn	ny	canyon

flavor and has a dark color. (The lighter olive oil is great for massage—try it; you may find the perfect mate just by your scent alone!)

BASIL
Basil is considered the king of all herbs, especially in Italian cooking. When mixed with fresh tomatoes, garlic, and olive oil it has no rival. If you add some parmesan and some pine nuts you have *Pesto*, that great aromatic pasta sauce. This is a specialty of the Genoese. Basil is one of the best herbs to promote digestion. You can grow it on your window sill. Give it plenty of warm light and water. The smell will stimulate your taste buds and you'll want to make fresh pasta sauce every day!

TOMATOES
Any fresh variety of tomato, preferably from one's own garden, is used in Italian cooking. In Italy they grow "plum" tomatoes (sometimes called *romano* in the U.S.) or the Marmande variety. These are the huge, curved, irregularly shaped tomatoes that have great flavor. Warm climate and healthy soil both lend themselves to a great tomato garden. That's why I like it here in Southern California. In New Jersey, they grow Beefsteak tomatoes, one of the most juicy, fattest, and reddest tomatoes in the country. It's worth a trip to New Jersey just to experience the taste. A salad of garden tomatoes and fresh mozzarella sprinkled with home-grown basil is "to die for."

PARMESAN CHEESE
Known in Italy as *grana* ("fine grain"), it is ideal for cooking with pasta. This is the cheese that was hanging in the Italian *grocerea* (markets) I passed every day on my way to school. Buy it by the chunk. Choose the kind that is about four years old, if you can find it. Store it in sheets of foil in the bottom of the fridge until ready to use.

PEPPERS
I vividly remember the times when my best friend, Franco, and I would sit at the kitchen table with my Grandfather Lo Russo and share a whole loaf (or two) of fresh Italian bread. We would eat the bread with *Pepperoncini*, those little Italian hot peppers that could burn the chrome off of any car's bumper. We would sit devouring a whole jar, our

mouths spitting fire and our tongues and lips so numb that the dentist could have extracted all our teeth and we wouldn't have felt any pain. They're Italian Novocain.

PASTAS

Bucatini are long, thick pasta.

Cannelloni are hollowed-out pasta tubes in the shape of "bagpipes," usually filled with tomato sauce.

Capellini (also called *fedilini* or *spaghettini*) is "fine-hair" pasta, usually coiled. Angel Hair is even thinner.

Cresti di galli is named for its resemblance to a "rooster's comb."

Ditalini are small macaroni cut into "little thimble" shapes.

Farfalle, known as bows in this country, look like "butterflies."

Funghini, used in soup, is in pasta's "mushroom" family."

Gnocci are little "dumpling-like" pastas.

Lumache resemble a "snail shell."

Occhi di Lupo are large tubes of macaroni, referred to as "wolf's eyes."

Orcchiette are shaped to resemble "ears."

Pulcini, used in soups, is from the "little chicken" family of pasta.

Ravioli are small cases of pasta, usually stuffed with meat, cheese, or vegetables.

Riccini are groove pasta, twisted into ringlet "curls."

Ruoti are round with spokes, resembling a "chariot wheel."

Tortellini are small rounds of stuffed pasta twisted into a shape resembling the Roman goddess Venus' navel.

Vermicelli is the southern Italian word for spaghetti and means "worms."

Zitti are a type of tubular macaroni "cut" into shorter lengths; often backed in tomato sauce.

CAFFÈ (Coffee)

My Grandfather Columbrito, Grandmother Grace's husband, was responsible for stimulating my interest and taste buds to that wonderful Italian beverage that looked like the oil my father would put in the car engine: espresso.

I would watch him on Sundays after church sitting at his kitchen table. He would take day-old Italian bread and carefully break off small pieces without dropping any crumbs on the floor, and submerge the bread into a cup of Italian coffee. He would spoon out the pieces of bread as if eating a bowl of coffee soup. When I partook of this custom I would load the coffee with lots of sugar and milk to cover the bitterness.

Espresso (8 tbs. of fine-ground Italian coffee and 1½ cups of water)

Cappuccino is named after the Cappuccines, a holy order of friars whose robes are the same color as the coffee (2⅔ cup of espresso, 1⅓ whole milk).

Caffè Latte (2 cups whole milk, 2 cups Italian-roast coffee)

Caffè Mocha is the same as caffè latte, but add chocolate powder or syrup.

Iced coffee—add milk and sugar to any of the above and add ice cubes.

Suggested Songs & Menus

O Sole Mio
Salad: Insalata di mozzarella, olivo, e rucolie (p. 42)
Main Dish: Fettuccine with fennel and arugula (p. 60)
Dessert: Crema caromella (p. 98)

Santa Lucia
Salad: Escarole with walnuts, celery, and parmesan (p. 45)
Main Dish: Trenette al salmon (p. 64)
Dessert: No-bake rum cake (p. 100)

Arriverderci Roma
Salad: Andy's Antipasta Salad (p. 46)
Main Dish: Grandma Grace's Eggplant Parmesan (p. 79)
Dessert: Anise Cookies (p. 100)

That's Amore
Salad: Insalata di arance e finocchi (p. 45)
Main Dish: That's Amore tomato and basil pasta (p. 66)
Dessert: Tirami-Su (p. 95)

Volare
Salad: Caprese/tomato and mozzarella slices (p. 31)
Main Dish: Volare vermicelli with watercress aglio-olio (p. 55)
Dessert: Neopolitan cheesecake (p. 106)

Martha
Salad: Insalata con lattuga e parmegiano (p. 40)
Main Dish: Pasta Penne Tetrazzini (p. 50)
Dessert: Biscotti Bambini (p. 97)

Non ti Scorda di me
Salad: Escarole orzo e garbanzo Menotti (p. 36)
Main Dish: Vermicelli alla puttanesca (p. 51)
Dessert: Italian pineapple ice with raspberrry kirsch (p. 104)

La Donna e Mobile
Salad: Insalata Verdi (p. 40)
Main Dish: Pasta Primavera (p. 52)
Dessert: Ricotta Puffs (p. 96)

Funiculi Funicula
Salad: Pasta e fagioli (p. 35)
Main Dish: Fettuccine with tuna, black olives, and capers (p. 54)
Dessert: Italian lemon sherbet (p. 107)

Torna a Surriento
Salad: Pavarotti's pasta salad (p. 44)
Main Dish: Pasta Puccini (p. 51)
Dessert: Summer Dolce (p. 103)

Antipasti

I'll bet you think antipasto means "after the pasta." Well, it means "before the meal." It's served like hors d'oeuvres. You can be as creative as you like with this course. My favorite antipasto dishes are the ones I have in this chapter. You can almost make a full meal out of this course. By adding a nice assortment of things—like mozzarella cheese balls, roasted eggplant, roasted peppers, fried and breaded zucchini, and marinated mushrooms—one can satisfy the most discerning taste buds and stimulate the palate for the feast to follow. You can combine a little of all of these recipes to make a great presentation at a party. Set it in the middle of the table, or have it just to snack on while you're watching all three of the *Godfather* movies, back to back. It's really an offer your guests can't refuse.

Some quick antipasti are:
- Bruschetta—toasted Italian bread, thickly sliced with garlic, virgin olive oil, salt, and pepper*
- Crostini—baked bread, cut small, with mozzarella cheese, anchovies, tomatoes, oregano, salt, and pepper*
- Funghi Marinata—marinated mushrooms
- Melanzone Marinata—marinated eggplant

* A spread of Kalamata olives, gorgonzola, and roasted peppers can be on both the bruschetta and crostini. Chop fine in food processor and sauté in olive oil; spread on bread!

A star (*) indicates a favorite recipe of the author's

Breaded Zucchini Sticks

    3 zucchinis
    ½ cup flour
    3 eggs, beaten (or substitute with yogurt)
    1 cup Italian bread crumbs
    1 cups water
    1 tsp. basil leaves
    Pinch of black pepper
    Olive oil

Quarter zucchini lengthwise and cut pieces into half. (For thinner slices, use largest special cutting blade on cheese grater.) In a bowl, combine the flour, bread crumbs, and eggs. Fill skillet with oil and heat. Dip zucchini pieces in batter and then into hot oil. Fry on all sides until tender and crisp. (Serves 4)

Deep-Fried Mozzarella

    Vegetable oil for deep frying
    8 oz. (or less) fresh mozzarella cheese
    2 eggs
    1 cup fine bread crumbs or Italian bread crumbs
    Parmesan cheese
    Fresh-ground pepper to taste
    Flour

Cut the mozzarella crosswise into ¼-inch slices about 2 to 2½ inches long. Should make about nine pieces. In a heavy pot, heat a half-inch-deep layer of vegetable oil to 375°. Pepper the mozzarella pieces and place flour on a plate. Beat eggs in a shallow bowl and place bread crumbs on another plate. Dredge cheese slices first in flour, dip floured cheese into egg, then dredge cheese in bread crumbs. Re-dip the slices into egg again. Deep-fry the slices in batches, about a minute per side, until brown and crisp, but before the melted cheese leaks out. Remove with a slotted spatula and drain on absorbent paper briefly. Serve immediately.

Garlic Spinach Balls

> 2 pkg. frozen chopped spinach (cooked and drained)
> 2 cups herb-seasoned stuffing mix
> 6 eggs beaten
> 2 onions, chopped fine
> ½ cup chopped parsley
> ¾ cup melted margarine or butter
> ½ cup parmesan cheese
> 2 minced garlic cloves
> ½ tbs. thyme
> 1 tsp. black pepper

Mix in a large bowl and refrigerate for 15 minutes. Make small balls, and flash freeze. Then bake in oven for 20 minutes at 375°F. (Makes sixty balls.)

Stuffed Mushrooms

> 24 large mushrooms
> 2 garlic cloves, minced
> ½ cup butter or margarine
> 1 cup soft bread crumbs
> Fresh crab (optional)
> ½ cup parmesan cheese
> ½ tsp. salt
> ¼ tsp. pepper
> 2 tbs. fresh parsley (chopped), or 1 tbs. dry parsley

Remove stems from mushrooms and chop stems fine. Sauté garlic in ¼ cup of butter or margarine. Add chopped stems, bread crumbs, crab, cheese, salt, pepper, and parsley. Sauté mushroom caps briefly in remaining butter or margarine. Fill caps with stuffing and place in shallow casserole. Bake at 350° for 10-15 minutes.

Fennel, Green Bean & Olives

1 lb. beans, trimmed
1 large fennel bulb (1 lb.)
2 tbs. olive oil
3 tbs. lemon juice
1 can flat anchovy filets, minced
1 clove garlic, crushed
¼ cup oil-cured black olives, pitted and quartered

Blanch the green beans in salt water until tender but still crisp (approx. 10 minutes). Cut fennel in half, then cut lengthwise in thin strips. Combine olive oil, lemon juice, anchovies, and garlic in salad bowl. Toss the fennel and beans in dressing. Add olives and grind pepper over the top.

*CAPRESE
Tomatoes & Mozzarella Slices with Fresh Basil

4 ripe tomatoes
1 lb. fresh mozzarella
Red wine vinegar
4-5 fresh basil leaves
Oregano (fresh or dried)

Cut and quarter tomatoes and mozzarella and put side-by-side on large plate. Sprinkle vinegar and oregano on top. Cut basil leaves to garnish.

MOZZARELLA ALLA CAPRESÈ
Mozzarella Capri-style

> 3 6-oz. rounds of fresh mozzarella
> 3 large tomatoes (8 oz. each)
> 2 tbs. virgin olive oil
> 2 tsp. fresh oregano, chopped
> ½ tsp. fresh ground pepper

Slice the mozzarella into six slices. Cut and core tomatoes into eight slices, and place on dish. Sprinkle each with olive oil, oregano, and pepper. Serve before the main meal with fresh Italian garlic bread.

PEPPERONI ARROSTO VIVALDI
Roasted Peppers

> 6-8 large peppers (red, green, yellow; sweet fryers cubanelles
>   are the best)
> 2 lemons
> 8 tbs. extra-virgin olive oil
> 2 cloves garlic
> Salt to taste

Roast the peppers in a pre-heated 400° oven for at least 45 minutes, or until blackened. Put under cold water to wash off blackened skin. Remove stems and seeds. Slice lengthwise (¼- to ½-inch wide strips) and place in deep dish. Marinade the peppers in the olive oil, garlic, and lemon juice (the longer the better). Serve with fresh Italian bread (bruschetta or crostini).

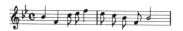

Zuppa

Someone once said: You can always tell if the main course is going to be a hit if the soup is good. In most cases, it's the truth. Next time you go out for dinner and the soup is not quite what you expected, especially if it's cold, you had better ask for the check and have the main course elsewhere.

I always enjoy my soup hot—not boiling, but palatable. This warms me up for the meal to follow. It says that the chef is concerned enough to pay attention to what is being served right from the start. It's like foreplay, preparing the family and the guests for what is to follow.

In this section I give you some of my favorite soup recipes. There are many more that complement the Italian meal, but these are the most loved and enjoyed by everyone. The Pasta Fagiole is a classic, real down-home, on-the-farm, Italian-style cooking at its best. The Minestrone is one of the soups that put a little bit of Italian in every household.

Remember—always have some fresh-grated parmesan cheese and some Italian bread on the table. They add so much to the enjoyment of the zuppa. Enjoy!

A star (*) indicates a favorite recipe of the author's

MINESTRONE

2 tbs. virgin olive oil
1 cup tomatoes, skinned and chopped
⅓ cup garbanzo beans (chick peas, soaked overnight)
¼ cup basil leaves
1 sprig parsley, chopped
9 cups water
1 carrot, peeled and diced
1 celery stalk, diced
1 cup potatoes, diced
1 large zucchini, diced
1 cup shredded cabbage
Salt to taste
Freshly ground pepper
½ cup barley
½ cup parmesan
½ tsp. hing (garlic substitute) or 3 cloves minced garlic

Heat oil in large saucepan, add cabbage and hing. Sauté for 1 minute. Add tomatoes, garbanzos, basil, parsley, and water. Bring to a boil, cover, and simmer for 1 hour. Add carrots and celery, and cook for 20 more minutes. Add remaining ingredients, except cheese. Cook 45 more minutes. Add salt to taste. Let soup stand for 15 minutes. Stir in parmesan cheese and serve hot. (Serves 6)

Zuppa

Vegetable Stock/Soup

2 large potatoes, unpeeled but quartered
2 large carrots, peeled, sliced thick
1 celery stalk, chopped
1 large red onion, peeled and quartered
1 bay leaf
12 peppercorns
10 cups water (2½ quarts)
Additional (optional): Garlic cloves, ginger, apples, pears
    (seeded and chopped).

Cook the ingredients in a large pot. Let simmer for 1½ hours. You can drain the vegetables and use the stock for risotto.

*PASTA E FAGIOLI

¾ lbs. dried pinto beans or white cannellone beans (soaked
    overnight) or garbanzo beans (chick peas)
1 medium onion, cut small
2 tbs. virgin olive oil
1 tbs. tomato paste or 4 stewed plum tomatoes
½ tsp. salt
Fresh-ground pepper to taste
¼ lb. *tagliolini* (thin long pasta) or small tube-shaped ziti or
    small shells or little elbows

Sauté onion in olive oil, add tomatoes and beans. Add water to cover 2 inches above bean level. Let simmer 2 hours. Add pasta and bring to boil. Make sure beans are well cooked before adding pasta. Add pasta and cook ingredients until done. Scoop out and serve with fresh parmesan cheese and Italian bread.

*Ida's Zucchini Zuppa

3 large zucchini, diced
½ onion
1 garlic clove minced
2 tbs. olive oil
3 fresh tomatoes
1 cup fresh basil leaves
1 tbs. oregano
Salt and pepper
10 cups water
Romano cheese

Lightly sauté the onion and garlic in olive oil. Cook zucchini in water, add tomatoes and the rest of the ingredients, and let simmer. Sprinkle fresh romano cheese on and serve with fresh-baked Italian bread.

*ESCAROLE ORZO and GARBANZO SOUP MENOTTI

8 cups homemade chicken stock
½ cup *orzo* pasta (or *pulcini*)
1 medium head escarole (1 lb.), washed
Fresh grated parmesan cheese
1 cup garbanzo beans (chick peas)

Heat broth in a large stock pot and bring to a boil. Add pasta and reduced to low boil. Cook for 5 minutes. (Skim off foam.) Add chick peas and let cook for 4 to 5 minutes more. Stack clean escarole leaves and chop into small pieces. Add to broth and cook, uncovered, at gentle simmer about 10 minutes. Serve with fresh grated parmesan cheese and black pepper.

CIOPPINO GIULIANI
Italian Bouillabaisse

4 mussels
2 clams
4 jumbo shrimp (peeled)
4 medium-large scallops
8 1-oz. pieces of whitefish
2 pieces of crab
3 oz. virgin olive oil
1 large sweet onion, chopped
1 large yellow bell pepper, chopped and seeded
2 celery stalks, chopped
3 large garlic cloves, crushed and chopped
4 oz. parsley, minced
8 oz. clam juice (optional)
4 oz. tomato paste
3½ cups of fresh tomatoes (canned, diced optional)
1 tsp. fresh oregano, chopped
1 tsp. fresh basil, chopped
2 dry red chilies, chopped (optional)
1 tsp. sugar
1 oz. Tabasco
Salt and black pepper to taste

In a two-quart pasta pot, sauté celery, onion, bell pepper, and garlic in olive oil for 5 minutes. Wash all the fish very well. Bring to boil. Add seafood and cook 20 minutes.

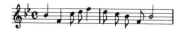

Insalata

Salads and Sunshine

I'VE ALWAYS LIKED sunshine and the color green. The grass around our house was always rich with color, especially in the summer. It was a real blessing to see summer roll around and watch our garden grow. My Grandfather Lo Russo seemed to practice magic when he brought the garden to life year after year. The best red tomatoes and the different varieties of lettuce, cucumbers, carrots, and beets would come right from the yard onto the dinner table.

In Italy, like much of Europe, salads are eaten at the end of the meal, particularly after the pasta. It helps digestion. Some people enjoy salad before the meal, or, like me, during. Whatever your choice, you should see greens on your table daily. *"Non giorno sensa verdura, non giorno sensa sole* (A day without greens is like a day without sunshine)."

With salads, remember that the key word is "fresh."

THE GREENER THE GREEN THE BETTER			
(Based on a 3.5 oz. serving)			
Green	*Vit. A*	*Vit. C*	*Calcium*
	(INT'L. UNITS)	(MG)	(MG)
Arugula	7,400	91	309
Spinach	6,715	28	99
Watercress	4,700	43	120
Chicory	4,000	24	100
Romaine	2,600	24	36
Red Leaf	1,900	18	68
Boston or Bibb	970	8	35
Iceberg	330	4	19

*INSALATA CON LATTUGA E PARMEGIANO
Green Salad with Parmesan Shavings

10 cups bite-size assorted greens: arugula, escarole, watercress,
and leaf lettuce, rinsed and dried.
¼ cup minced fresh basil and parsley
2 tbs. white-wine vinegar or balsamic vinegar
Salt and pepper to taste
⅓ cup extra virgin olive oil
4 oz. parmesan cheese, shaved into curls

Combine salad greens in bowl with parsley. Whisk vinegar with salt
and pepper and add oil. Toss salad with dressing and serve with
shaved parmesan cheese.

INSALATA VERDI
Green Salad

1 head of escarole
1 head of chicory
1 head of romaine lettuce
2 tbs. olive oil
1 tbs. balsamic vinegar
1 cup garlic-flavored croutons
Salt and pepper

Cut and wash all lettuce, then dry in salad spinner. Mix olive oil and
balsamic vinegar with salt and fresh ground pepper to taste. Add
garlic croutons.

Fennel, Celery & Parsley Salad with Shaved Romano & Parmesan

2¼ cup thinly sliced fennel
2¼ cup thinly sliced celery
1¼ cup minced fresh parsley
Pepper
Shaved romano and parmesan to taste
Balsamic vinegar and olive oil

Toss the fennel, celery, and parsley. Serve with balsamic vinegar and olive oil. Add fresh pepper to taste. Sprinkle with shaved romano and parmesan cheeses.

Fennel & Orange Salad with Shaved Pecorino and Parmesan

6 medium sweet oranges (seedless and peeled)
6 medium fennel bulbs (trimmed and cored)
1 lb. black olives (Kalamata, Greek)
2 tbs. balsamic vinegar
Shaved parmesan and romano cheeses
Fresh-ground black pepper
Olive oil

Deseed, peel, and cut oranges into quarters. Arrange on a dish next to fennel bulbs, trimmed and cored in sections. Pit and cut olives into quarters and place on dish around the outside of the oranges. Add olive oil and vinegar and shaved cheese.

*INSALATA DI MOZZARELLA, OLIVO E RUCOLA
Mozzarella Salad with Black Olives and Arugula

1 lb. fresh mozzarella cheese (soft or buffalo cheese)
⅔ cup Sicilian black olives or Kalamata, halved
2 large heads of arugula, trimmed, washed, and torn
9 tbs. virgin olive oil
¼ cup aged Balsamic vinegar
Salt and fresh-ground pepper to taste

Cube the mozzarella and mix with all the ingredients in a bowl. Serve with fresh toasted Italian garlic bread.

Eggplant Salad

2 lbs. small eggplant
⅓ cup virgin olive oil
¼ cup chopped parsley
½ tsp. salt
2 tsp. minced fresh ginger
2 tsp. sugar (turbinado preferred)
2 tsp. lemon juice

Preheat oven to 400°. Prick the eggplants with a fork and bake in oven until very tender (about 30 minutes). When they are done, cut in half lengthwise and remove seeds. Scoop out the pulp from the skin and place in a sieve to drain. When the eggplant is drained, put in large bowl and mash with a wooden spoon. Add the remaining ingredients, mix well, and chill for a few hours. Serve on a lettuce leaf surrounded by tomato wedges and olives. (Serves 4)

Vegetable Salad

 1 8-oz. can pitted olives (Greek or Italian)
 1 16-oz. can water-packed artichoke hearts
 ½ lb. hard Italian cheese cut in ½-inch slices
 3 medium tomatoes, cut in eighths
 3 tbs. olive oil
 1½ tsp. lemon juice
 2 tsp. chopped fresh basil leaves
 ½ tsp. black pepper
 Pinch of hing (garlic replacement) or 2 cloves minced garlic

In a bowl, combine ingredients and set in refrigerator for one hour before serving. (Serves 4)

Dilled Cucumber and Beet Salad

 1 bunch beets, washed
 2 cucumbers, peeled, halved, and seeded
 1 cup yogurt
 2 tsp. fresh dill, minced (or 1 tsp. dried)
 Fresh dill sprig for garnish
 Pinch of salt

Roast the beets in a shallow roasting pan at 325° (about 35 minutes). Remove skins. Cool and slice paper-thin. Add cucumbers. Mix the yogurt and salt and pour over the beets and cucumbers.

Tortellini with Roasted Walnuts

½ cup roasted walnuts
⅓ cup walnut oil
3 tbs. wine vinegar
Salt and pepper to taste
2 tbs. olive oil
2 cloves garlic, minced
⅓ cup green pepper
¼ cup red and yellow bell peppers
¼ cup red onion, diced
1 rib celery, diced
½ cup parmesan, finely grated
12 oz. tortellini
Parsley

Whisk together the walnut oil, and vinegar, with salt and pepper to taste. Sauté the garlic in the olive oil. Cook several minutes until golden brown. Drain on paper towel. Cook the tortellini al dente. In a bowl, put tortellini, parsley, and the peppers, onion, and celery. Pour the dressing and add walnuts and parmesan.

*Pavarroti's Pasta Salad

1 lb. curly pasta (carrot, spinach, tomato, or small shells)
16 oz. Greek Kalamata olives, quartered
2 tbs. olive oil
½ cup light white vinegar
2-4 fresh garden tomatoes, diced
½ bunch fresh parsley
1 each yellow and red bell pepper, diced
½ tsp. white or black pepper

Cook the pasta al dente, add the ingredients and mix well. Put into refrigerator and serve chilled.

Escarole with Walnuts, Celery, and Parmesan

2 heads escarole
½ cup celery heart, sliced thin
¼ lb. parmesan, sliced thin
⅓ cup walnuts, broken
1 can anchovy filets, finely chopped
¾ cup olive oil
¼ cup lemon juice or red-wine vinegar
2 tbs. parsley, minced
Ground pepper

Wash the escarole and combine celery, parmesan, and walnuts. Whisk together anchovies, olive oil, lemon juice or red-wine vinegary, parsley and ground pepper. Pour over salad.

INSALATA DI ARANCE E FINOCCHI
Orange and Fennel Salad

3 medium to large fennel bulbs
3 tbs. extra virgin olive oil
Salt and pepper to taste
2 medium oranges

Cut and core the fennel into thin slices. Let sit in olive oil, salt, and pepper for at least 10 minutes (the longer the better). Peel one orange and cut into thin round slices (save the juice). Drain oil from fennel and mix with the juice of the other orange to make a cream sauce. Pour the rest of the juice over the top of the fennel and garnish with the sliced orange and serve. This is also great for after dinner.

*Andy's Antipasta Salad

½ cup gorgonzola cheese cut in small chunks
½ cup fresh mozzarella cheese balls
Fontana cheese
Italian bread, cut, in bread basket
Cruets of virgin and fruit-flavored olive oil, red-wine vinegar,
    and balsamic vinegar
Small lemon wedges
Roasted peppers
Italian pepperoncini (small hot peppers)

Serve before the meal.

*QUICK PASTA SALADS

The Mediterranean

Egg, tomato, and spinach pasta with red bell peppers, black olives, and romano cheese.

The Palermo

Egg, tomato and spinach pasta, with artichoke hearts, anchovies, and capers.

The Isle of Capri

Carrot, spinach, and egg pasta, with small bay shrimp, lemon wedges, and Greek olives.

All the above pasta salads can be dressed with Italian poppy-seed dressing.

Pasta e Salsa

Pasta and Sauces

Someone told me that the pasta consumption in the U.S. is 18.4 pounds per person (1990). In Italy, the average is 60 pounds per person!

One should eat about three grams of carbohydrates per pound of body weight each day. Between 55 and 70 percent of all calories should come from carbohydrates.

Southern Italians, it is said, became the masters of homemade pastas. The warm, dry climate in the south favored the drying of freshly made pasta, cooked *al dente* ("to the tooth," i.e., requires chewing).

BASIC SAUCE

Combine chopped tomatoes with sliced or chopped black or green olives, garlic, and fresh herbs (basil, oregano, parsley). Mix in virgin olive oil, garlic, and dried red chili peppers. Pour over and mix into cooked pasta.

QUICK SAUCE

Butter, olive oil, chopped parsley, and basil, salt and pepper, and grated parmesan and romano cheeses. Warm in saucepan and pour over pasta.

A star (*) indicates a favorite recipe of the author's

*Marinara Sauce Martinelli

    3 tbs. virgin olive oil
    1 onion, minced
    1 carrot, minced
    1 celery rib, minced
    3 garlic cloves, minced
    6 fresh basil leaves
    ¼ cup fresh parsley, minced
    6 cups plum tomatoes, fresh peeled, or canned

Heat olive oil and sauté garlic and onions. Add the rest of the ingredients and simmer to taste. Keep covered and refrigerate until needed.

> *Per serving . . . Calories: 390   Fat: 10.86   Carbohydrates: 16.99*

*PASTA PENNE TETRAZZINI

    1 lb. penne pasta (tube-shaped)
    2 tbs. virgin olive oil
    1 16-oz. can Kalamata (Greek) olives, quartered
    2 sticks butter, melted
    1 bunch fresh parsley, minced
    4 medium fresh tomatoes, quartered
    ½ cup fresh parmesan and romano, grated
    3 garlic gloves, chopped

In a large saucepan, heat oil, sauté garlic until brown. Add olives and tomatoes and cover. In separate pan, melt butter, add cheese, and let simmer over low heat. Cook pasta *al dente*, drain, and put into large pasta bowl. Mix in the olive oil sauce and pour in the melted butter and cheese. Add the minced parsley just before serving. Toss well and serve.

> *Per serving . . . Calories: 441.25 Fat: 41.51   Carbohydrates: 25.92*

*VERMICELLI ALLA PUTTANESCA
Vermicelli Streetwalker-style

1 garlic clove
2 tbs. olive oil
6 anchovy filets
3 tbs. capers
Fresh-ground pepper
3 tbs. toasted bread crumbs
24 pitted Sicilian-style black olives (not dried)
¼ cup fresh parsley
1 cup plum tomatoes, peeled and chopped
1¼ lb. vermicelli

Cook vermicelli. Sauté garlic in olive oil until golden brown. Chop anchovies, capers, olives, parsley, and add to olive oil. Add tomatoes and bring to simmer. Cook 8-10 minutes. Remove from heat. Pour sauce over pasta, sprinkle with bread crumbs, toss, and serve.

Per serving . . . Calories: 421.12 Fat: 29.54 Carbohydrates: 23.89

*PASTA PUCCINI
Angel Hair Pasta with Tomatoes and Fresh Shittake Mushrooms

1 14.5-0z. can of stewed tomatoes
2 tbs. olive oil
3 cloves of garlic, minced
1 medium onion, finely chopped
1 medium bell pepper, diced
1 medium yellow bell pepper, diced
½ cup dry red wine
4 oz. mushrooms, chopped

Sauté garlic in olive oil. Add onion and simmer. Stir in tomatoes, add wine and cover for 10 minutes. Add bell peppers and mushrooms, cook another 10 minutes. Pour over *cappellini* (angel hair) pasta.

Per serving . . . Calories: 239 Fat: 7.62 Carbohydrates: 34.89

PASTA PRIMAVERA

2 tbs. olive oil
1 large onion
2 cups peeled eggplant
2 medium zucchini, diced
1 medium yellow bell pepper, chopped
2 large tomatoes, chopped
3 cloves garlic, minced
1½ cups tomato juice
½ cup fresh basil, minced
¼ cup cream or half-and-half
½ cup parmesan cheese
Fettuccine or linguine pasta

In cast-iron skillet, sauté onion, eggplant, zucchini, bell pepper, to-matoes, and garlic in olive oil. Add tomato juice and bring to simmer, covered, for 10 minutes. Add basil and cook a few more minutes, until vegetables are tender. Cook the pasta *al dente.* Stir half-and-half into vegetables. Add parmesan and spoon over the pasta.

Per serving... Calories: 286   Fat: 24.99   Carbohydrates: 38.21

SPAGHETTI AL PISELLI E PANNA
Spaghetti with Peas and Cream

10 oz. fresh or frozen peas
1 small onion, chopped
2 tbs. olive oil
1 tbs. butter
½ cup water
¼ cup heavy cream
¾-1 cup sour cream
½ tsp. ground black pepper
16 oz. spaghetti or rigatoni

In the oil and butter, cook onion. Add ½ cup water and bring to a boil. Add peas and cook a few minutes. Make sure the water covers just above the peas. Cook about 5 minutes more. Stir in heavy cream and sour cream. Add salt and pepper. Serve over spaghetti or rigatoni.

Per serving . . . Calories: 589   Fat: 60.63   Carbohydrates: 24.17

PENNE AL QUATTRO FORMAGGI

4 oz. fontana cheese
4 oz. provoletta cheese
4 oz. gouda cheese, grated
2 oz. parmesan cheese, grated
(or any mellow soft cheese at room temperature)
½ tsp. ground pepper
Fresh parsley sprigs (garnish)
16. oz. penne or mostaccioli rigati

Mix the cheese (having kept them at room temperature) on a large serving plate. Sprinkle with black pepper and add pasta while still hot. Garnish with fresh parsley.

Per serving . . . Calories: 497   Fat: 32.23   Carbohydrates: 18.69

Fettuccine with Tuna, Black Olives, and Capers

3 cups marinara sauce, fresh
1 cup sliced black olives
6 tbs. capers, drained
1 6.5-oz. can tuna (packed in oil), drained
1½ lb. fettucine
2 tbs. unsalted butter
Fresh grated parmesan cheese
Cayenne pepper to taste

Cook the fresh marinara sauce. Add tuna (cut into small chunks), olives, and capers. Let simmer. Cook the fettuccine *al dente* and toss in sauce pan. Sprinkle with parmesan and serve.

Per serving . . . Calories: 226   Fat: 6.61   Carbohydrates: 20.13

Penne with Mixed Grilled Vegetables

6 large slices of zucchini, cut diagonally
6 thick slices of eggplant, peeled
3 medium red and yellow bell peppers, quartered lengthwise
3 medium leeks, washed and blanched
1 tbs. virgin olive oil
1½ lbs. pasta, penne ragati
Balsamic vinegar

Sprinkle eggplant with salt and let dry for 30 minutes. Cut leeks and brush with olive oil. Place zucchini and peppers on grill and cook 4-5 minutes on each side. Grill eggplant and cut vegetables in chunks. Cook penne *al dente*. Sprinkle vegetables with balsamic vinegar and mix pasta with vegetables in pasta bowl. (Serves 6)

Per serving . . . Calories: 245   Fat: 4.85   Carbohydrates: 42.95

*VOLARE VERMICELLI
Vermicelli with Watercress Aglio-Olio

1 lb. vermicelli (imported)
2 tbs. garlic, minced
1 tsp. salt
1 cup chicken stock or water
2 cups watercress, chopped
2 tbs. extra virgin olive oil

Bring 5 quarts of water to a boil. Heat olive oil and garlic and sauté until golden brown. Add salt and chicken stock to boiling water, then pasta. Stir oil and garlic and watercress into drained pasta.

Per serving ... Calories: 90.75 Fat: 0.78   Carbohydrates: 16.88

PESTO

3 cups (firmly packed) basil leaves
2 large cloves garlic
2 tbs. parmesan cheese, grated
⅞ cup olive oil
¼ cup pine nuts

Blend together all ingredients in a food processor or blender. Add pine nuts and blend for 10 seconds. This can be frozen and used for many different pasta dishes.

Per serving ... Calories: 593   Fat: 61.45   Carbohydrates: 3.40

Fusilli Bucatti Pasta with Fresh Green Beans, Tomatoes & Basil

1 lb. fusilli bucatti pasta (corkscrew)
1½ lb. green beans, cut in half
1 large tomatoes, chopped
2 tbs. olive oil
½ tsp. salt
¼ tsp. fresh ground pepper
1 tbs. fresh basil
1 tsp. oregano
1 clove garlic
Parmesan and Romano

Heat oil in skillet, add garlic. Stir in tomatoes, then add beans. Cover with water, add salt and pepper, bring to a boil, cover and lower heat. Simmer for 15 minutes or until beans are tender. Remove cover and increase heat to thicken the liquid. Cook pasta *al dente*. Pour sauce over drained pasta and mix well. Serve with fresh basil, grated parmesan and romano cheeses.

Per serving . . . Calories: 227   Fat: 14.01   Carbohydrates: 23.53

PASTA LA SCALA
Penne with Broccoli-Rabe (rapini)

1 lb. broccoli-rabe
1 lb. penne pasta
2 tbs. virgin olive oil
2 garlic cloves, crushed
2 tbs. onion, minced
3 anchovy filets, cut into pieces
¼ cup dry white wine
¼ tsp. hot red pepper flakes
3 plum tomatoes, peeled, seeded, and diced
¼ cup light cream
Parmesan cheese, freshly grated

Trim the broccoli-rabe and cut into 1-inch pieces. Put into boiling water and cover pot. When water returns to a boil, drain broccoli and rinse well with cold water. Heat oil in a large skillet over medium heat, add garlic, and cook until it just begins to turn golden. Remove and discard garlic. Add onion to oil and sauté until soft, about 2 minutes. Add anchovies and stir until they dissolve. Add wine and boil until almost evaporated. Sprinkle pepper flakes in the tomatoes and cook, stirring, 3 to 4 minutes until tomatoes have softened, but have not yet fallen apart. Add cream, turn up heat, add broccoli rabe. Toss to coat it well with the sauce. Cook the penne pasta about 8 minutes or until *al dente*. Mix the sauce over drained pasta and serve with grated cheese.

Per serving ... Calories: 409   Fat: 29.96   Carbohydrates: 31.50

PASTA RIGOLETTO DEL MAR ALA VERDURA
Capellini with Shrimp and Asparagus

1 lb. shrimp (medium-size; cleaned and peeled)
1 medium onion, chopped
2 cloves garlic, minced
2 tbs. virgin olive oil
2 cups fresh or canned plum tomatoes, chopped
1 tsp. fresh thyme leaves
½ tsp. hot pepper flakes
1 lb. asparagus
1 lb. capellini (angel hair) pasta
2 tbs. Italian parsley, chopped

In a skillet, soften the onion and garlic in the olive oil. Add tomatoes, thyme, and pepper flakes, and simmer gently, covered, for 15 minutes. Add water if the sauce gets too thick. Slice the asparagus into 2-inch pieces. Place in a steamer and steam until bright green, but still *al dente*. Boil the water and cook the pasta *al dente*. Add the shrimp to the sauce and cook for 2 minutes. Add asparagus and cook for 1 more minute. Place in heated bowl and mix everything together. Serve and sing!

Per serving . . . Calories: 216   Fat: 13.29   Carbohydrates: 11.96

PASTA SICILIANA CON LE SARDE
Pasta with Sardines

1½ lb. fresh sardines (small)
1 lb. wild fennel
3 tbs. virgin olive oil
1 large onion
5 salted anchovies, or 10 filets, chopped
⅛ tsp. saffron
1¾ oz. sultana raisins (soaked in water)
⅓ cup pine nuts
Salt and pepper to taste
1 lb. bucatini pasta
⅓-oz. can almonds (peeled and roasted)
1 cup Italian bread crumbs
2 lemons

Filet and clean the sardines. Clean and cut the fennel. Cook fennel in salt water (reuse the water for pasta). Drain and chop fine in food processor. In olive oil, cook onion till transluscent (5 min.) and add half of sardines chopped. Add chopped anchovies, fennel, saffron, drained raisins, pine nuts, almonds, salt, and pepper. Cook pasta "al dente" and add all ingredients to oven-proof dish. Add toasted bread crumbs and toss. Cut one lemon in slices and garnish the caserole dish. Squeeze the remaining lemon over the dish and bake in a 300° oven for 20-25 minutes.

Per serving . . . Calories: 641   Fat: 56.25   Carbohydrates: 30.65

Fettuccine with Fennel and Arugula

1 bunch arugula
1 bulb fresh fennel
3 tbs. extra-virgin olive oil
3 scallions, chopped
2 garlic cloves, minced
1 cup tomatoes (peeled, finely chopped, fresh or canned)
12-oz. fresh fettuccine
Fresh parmesan or romano, freshly grated
Salt and pepper to taste

Rinse and drain the arugula. Discard the stems and set leaves aside. Cut tops off fennel bulb and discard the stems. Cut the bulb into very thin slices and set aside. Heat oil in a large skillet and sauté scallions until tender. Stir in garlic, sliced fennel, and continue to sauté until tender. Add tomatoes and cook about 10 minutes. Add arugula and toss. Season to taste with salt and pepper. Remove from heat. Cook pasta and drain. Reheat the sauce and toss with fettuccine in a warmed serving bowl. Sprinkle with minced fennel tops and serve with parmesan or romano cheese.

Per serving . . . Calories: 305   Fat: 20.11   Carbohydrates: 12.33

Tosca Tortellini in Cream Sauce

1 lb. cheese tortellini
½ cup (1 stick) butter
1 tsp. red pepper flakes
1 cup fresh or whole canned tomatoes
¾ cup parmesan cheese, grated coarsely
1 cup heavy cream
Basil and garlic (optional)

Cook the tortellini and drain well. Put into large serving bowl. Melt butter in saucepan over medium heat. Sprinkle with crushed red pepper flakes. Simmer, then add the tomatoes, basil, and grated cheese. Simmer for three more minutes. Add heavy cream and cook another minute. Remove the sauce from the heat and pour over the tortellini. Serve and sing!

Per serving . . . Calories: 604   Fat: 52.22   Carbohydrates: 21.28

Penne Pagliacci with Roasted Asparagus and Pignoli with Garlic Crumbs

1 lb. fresh asparagus
1 lb. penne pasta
2 tbs. virgin olive oil
2 thin slices prosciutto ham (optional)
1 tbs. pignoli (pine nuts), lightly toasted
½ cup coarse bread crumbs (make from day-old Italian bread)
1 garlic clove, crushed
Parmigiano-Reggiano cheese, grated

Heat oven to 425°. Place asparagus in baking dish, sprinkle with 1 tbs. olive oil and the prosciutto (if desired). Blend and roast 10 minutes. Remove from oven and season with salt and fresh-ground pepper. Toast pignoli and set aside. In a medium skillet, combine 1 tbs. olive oil, bread crumbs, and crushed garlic. Cook mixture over low heat, stirring until golden. Boil pasta *al dente* about 12 minutes. Ladle out ½ cup of pasta liquid and reserve. Drain pasta. In a large bowl, toss the pasta, asparagus mixture, reserved pasta cooking liquid, and grated cheese. Top with the pignoli and garlic bread crumbs. Serve with extra cheese.

Per serving ... Calories: 165   Fat: 54.65   Carbohydrates: 6.09

Fettuccine with Asparagus
(Smoked salmon optional)

½ lb. fresh asparagus
1 tbs. butter
3 shallots, minced
1 cup heavy cream (or half & half)
4 oz. smoked salmon (sliced ¼-inch thick)
Fresh ground pepper to taste
1 tsp. fresh lemon juice
12 oz. fresh green fettuccine
2 tbs. fresh green dill, minced

Cut and peel asparagus on a slant, approx. 1-inch long. Steam until just tender (still bright green), about 3 minutes. Drain and set aside on paper towels. Boil water for pasta. Melt butter in large heavy skillet, add shallots and sauté until soft, but not brown. Stir in cream and simmer about 5 minutes or until cream thickens. Add asparagus and toss with sauce. Season with pepper and lemon juice. Cook pasta. While pasta drains, reheat the sauce. Add salmon. Toss pasta with sauce and mix well. Serve in a beautiful Italian pasta dish. Sprinkle with fresh minced dill.

Per serving . . . Calories: 488.3 Fat: 70.7 Carbohydrates: 18.99

TRENETTE AL SALMON
Linquine and Salmon

    6 oz. smoked salmon, cut small
    4 tbs. butter
    1 tbs. olive oil
    ½ onion, cut small
    1 cup heavy cream (or half & half)
    ½ tsp. fresh-grated black pepper
    16 oz. linguine

Cook onions in butter and oil until aroma bursts forth, then add cream and pepper on low heat. Add salmon and simmer a few more minutes. Mix into linguine.

Per serving . . . Calories: 823   Fat: 30.16   Carbohydrates: 19.23

Tuna Piano Pasta with Pomadoro Sauce

    1 12-oz. can tuna
    1 tbs. pine nuts
    1 tbs. currants
    1 garlic clove, minced
    4 sprigs parsley, cut fine
    ½ tsp. pepper, fresh ground
    16 oz. pasta, spaghetti or rigatoni
    2½ cups tomato sauce with parsley

Heat tomato sauce, add all ingredients except parsley. Let stand 30 minutes before mixing with pasta, then add parsley.

Per serving . . . Calories: 200   Fat: 4.21   Carbohydrates: 22.58

*Fettuccine with Artichoke Hearts

  1 pack artichoke hearts (water-packed or frozen) or 1 jar
  2 tbs. extra virgin olive oil
  2 garlic cloves, minced
  4 oz. fresh mushrooms, sliced
  Salt and pepper to taste
  2 tbs. Italian parsley, finely minced
  12 oz. fresh fettuccine
  Fresh parmesan, grated

Spread out artichoke hearts to dry on paper towels. Add 3 tbs. of olive oil to large skillet. Sauté garlic over medium heat for a few seconds. Increase heat, add artichoke hearts, and sauté for a few minutes, until lightly browned. Remove hearts from pan and drain well. Add another tbs. of oil to pan and brown mushrooms in high heat. Return the artichoke hearts to pan, season with salt and pepper, stir in parsley and remain oil. Cook fettuccine. While pasta drains, reheat sauce. Mix well in serving bowl, topped with cheese.

Per serving . . . Calories: 571   Fat: 26.71   Carbohydrates: 15.84

*Peas and Pasta Verdi

  1 large onion
  1 tsp. garlic, chopped
  2 tbs. virgin olive oil
  ¼ cup chopped basil
  1 can peas (fresh, if in season)
  1 lb. elbow macaroni

In saucepan, sauté ingredients (except the peas and macaroni) until golden brown. Add peas and sauté on low flame 5 minutes. Set aside. Cook macaroni in salted water. Reserve 2 cups of the water, then drain. Add macaroni to peas and mix well. If too dry, add water to loosen the macaroni. Remember, though, the drier the better. (Serves 6)

Per serving . . . Calories: 258   Fat: 42.93   Carbohydrates: 21.68

PASTA PINOLTA
Pasta with Pine Nuts

1 lb. #10 or #12 spaghetti
½ cup pine nuts (pinoltas)
2 tbs. olive oil
¼ cup red wine or balsamic vinegar
1 lb. green or black olives, pitted and quartered
½ cup bacon-flavored bits
2 garlic cloves, minced
Parsley and basil

Sauté garlic in olive oil, then add vinegar to taste, pine nuts, olives, and bacon bits. Cook and drain pasta, add to sauce and mix well. Serve hot. Top with springs of parsley and basil.

Per serving... Calories: 427   Fat: 31.64   Carbohydrates: 25.07

*That's Amore Tomato and Basil Pasta

1 lb. linguine or cappelini (angel hair) pasta
4 fresh tomatoes, quartered
2 tbs. virgin olive oil
3 garlic cloves
1 bunch fresh basil, diced
½ cup half-and-half

Cook pasta. Sauté garlic until brown in olive oil. Stir in cream or use ricotta cheese. Drain pasta and mix with sauce and tomatoes and basil.

Per serving... Calories: 605.3 Fat: 19.23   Carbohydrates: 22.70

*PASTA FANTASTICO LO RUSSO

1 lb. #10 pasta or linguine
1 lb. (16 oz.) Kalamata olives, quartered
3 tbs. virgin olive oil
3 tbs. red-wine-garlic or balsamic vinegar
2 oz. (½-cup) sun-dried tomatoes (dry or water-packed)
1 bunch Italian parsley, diced
16 oz. artichoke hearts (in water), quartered
4 fresh medium tomatoes, quartered (optional)
3 cloves garlic, minced
White pepper

Sauté garlic, olives, and artichoke hearts in olive oil. After steaming the sun-dried tomatoes (if they are dry), put them in. Cook pasta *al dente,* drain and mix together with sauce in large pan. Add vinegar and mix well. Cover and let simmer over low heat for about 5 minutes more. Add white pepper to taste and serve hot. Garnish with parsley.

Per serving . . . Calories: 277   Fat: 13.66   Carbohydrates: 37.95

Tortellini in Cheese Sauce

1 lb. tortellini
6 oz. Neufchatel cheese (room temp.)
6 oz. frozen spinach, chopped
1 tbs. butter
1 large red/yellow bell pepper, diced
1 medium onion, diced
¼ lb. mushrooms, sliced thinly
2 garlic cloves, minced
1 medium tomato, diced
¼ cup parmesan cheese, grated fine
1¼ tbs. capers, drained and minced
½ tsp. oregano (dried)
Basil

Boil the tortellini. Sauté in butter the garlic, peppers, onions, and mushrooms. Add Neufchatel cheese, spinach, and tomato. Blend well. Mix in parmesan, capers, oregano, and basil. Simmer the mix. Add tortellini to sauce and serve.

Per serving... Calories: 266   Fat: 15.18   Carbohydrates: 37.37

Bucatini with Black Pepper, Italian Bread crumbs, and Pecorino

2 tbs. virgin olive oil
4 tbs. (½ stick) unsalted butter
1 cup hard pecorino cheese, grated
1 tbs. fresh-ground pepper
1 lb. bucatini pasta
1 cup toasted Italian seasoned bread crumbs
1 garlic clove, crushed

Heat olive oil and butter. Cook pasta *al dente*. Pour oil and butter over the pasta and toss. Add cheese and pepper. Sprinkle with Italian bread crumbs.

Per serving... Calories: 539   Fat: 40.23   Carbohydrates: 21.15

RAVIOLLI DEL MAR
Raviolli with crab

FILLING
¾ lb. crab meat (fresh or frozen)
3 scallions
⅓ cup ricotta cheese (3 oz.) (see page 88)
salt and pepper to taste

PASTA DOUGH
2½ cups flour
2 or 3 eggs
1 tbs. vegetable oil
1 tsp. salt

SAUCE
Saffron threads
4 tbs. boiling water
1 cup unsalted butter
2 shallots, chopped
1 tbs. heavy cream

MAKING RAVIOLLIS
Sift flour onto a clean surface. Make a well inside the flour, into which mix the oil, eggs, and salt. Mix together by hand (a food processor takes less time). If the dough is sticky, add more flour. Shape the dough into a ball, then cut in half. Place half on floured work surface and knead until dough is elastic. Repeat with other half. Place balls into a bowl and refrigerate for an hour.

Sprinkle work surface with flour and roll out the dough with a rolling pin to the thickness of a postcard. The dough should look like velvet. Hang the dough over a broomstick or let it flop over the counter or table for 5–10 minutes. Cut the dough in two rectangular pieces. Using a small section at a time, brush with water and put a spoonful of filling on the dough in rows about two inches apart. Leave half an inch on each side. When you have two even rows of filling, cover with the other piece of dough and press down around each mound of filling, being sure to let the air out of each. Seal the edges. Using a pasta wheel or chef's knife, cut into 1½-inch or 4-inch squares. Lay the raviolli on floured kitchen towel and let dry for about two hours.

Boil water and drop in the raviolli. Cook 4–5 minutes, stirring with wooden spoon to prevent breaking. When finished cooking, the raviolli should float to the top

SAUCE

Boil saffron in a little water for 10 minutes. Add butter and heavy cream and let simmer. Add the shallots. Pour over raviolli and serve immediately.

Per serving . . . Calories: 379.67 Fat: 17.14   Carbohydrates: 26.89

Raviolli with Spinach and Cheese

FILLING
1 lb. fresh spinach (or frozen)
2 tbs. unsalted butter
⅓ cup fresh grated parmesan cheese
⅓ cup romano or pecorino cheese
1 large egg yolk
½ lb. ricotta (or use the recipe in this book)

SAUCE
3 tbs. unsalted butter
¾ cup heavy cream
3 oz. mild gorgonzola cheese
¼ cup grated parmesan (optional)
Parsley

Steam spinach and cut into small pieces. In a small skillet add butter and put in spinach. Let simmer 1–3 minutes. Put into mixing bowl and add parmesan, romano, riccotta, and egg yolk. Refrigerate for an hour.

See previous recipe for making raviolli dough.

Melt butter in saucepan, add gorgonzola and parmesan cheese. Stir in heavy cream. Let simmer. Pour over raviollis and garnish with sprigs of fresh parsley.

Use a simple garlic butter sauce as an optional treat. Garnish with fresh basil or parsley. Adding chopped fresh tomatoes to the sauce will make this dish extra special.

Per serving . . . Calories: 489   Fat: 17   Carbohydrates: 34.97

Specialità

Every so often a recipe comes along at a party or a special event that you just have to have for yourself. In this section I've included some of those recipes. The Stuffed Artichoke, Calamati Genoese, and especially the Eggplant Parmesan are just a few of those dishes that will keep them coming back for more.

Recipes that have been in the family for many years have a lot of good in them. Some of the ingredients may have changed over the years, but the main parts are still the same. When we share these cherished dishes, it's like opening a box of the family jewels and giving each guest a sample to enjoy for a little while. That's what Specialità is all about. Enjoy these gems, from our family to yours. If you don't have a special occasion, make up one! After all, life is to enjoy everyday—and everyday is a special event.

*CRESPELLE
Momma D's Manicotte

Crêpes:
>   4 eggs
>   1½ cups white flour (unbleached)
>   2⅔ cups milk and water
>   1-2 tbs. vegetable oil or melted butter
>   Pinch of salt

Sauce: (Follow basic marinara recipe)

Filling:
>   3 tbs. olive oil
>   2 cups chopped onion
>   3 large garlic cloves, minced
>   10 oz. fresh spinach (4 cups) or 10 oz. frozen
>   ½ cup basil
>   2 cups mozzarella cheese, grated (½ lb.)
>   ½ cup sharp parmesan and pecorino (grated)
>   3 lbs. ricotta cheese
>   Nutmeg
>   Salt and pepper to taste

To make the *crêpes,* beat the eggs, add oil, salt, and flour until smooth. Add milk and water and blend by hand-blender or food processor. Set aside for 30 minutes.

Heat a small skillet or crêpe pan (I prefer cast-iron). Brush bottom with oil. Pour small of amount of batter (I use a shot glass) into the pan, enough just to cover the bottom. Add milk or water to batter if too thick. Cook one side for 1 minute, then turn over until just lightly browned. Make as many as you can and stack on a plate. Cover with a cloth.

Prepare the *sauce* in a saucepan. Cook about 10 minutes. Be sure to prepare it thin.

To prepare the *filling,* heat olive oil in a large skillet. Sauté onions and garlic. Add chopped spinach and basil; cook until spinach is soft. Combine all the cheese in a large mixing bowl, and stir in some nutmeg, salt and pepper. Add to the onion and spinach mix.

Preheat oven to 375°. Spread some of the sauce over the bottom of a shallow baking dish. Place a large spoonful or two of the filling on each manicotti and roll it up. Place the filled crêpes in a single layer, close together, in the pan. Cover with more sauce and cheese and bake for 30 minutes, or until heated all the way through.

Stuffed Zucchini

6 medium zucchinis, sliced in half lengthwise
¼ cup rice
½ cup water
2 tbs. butter
¼ tsp. hing (garlic substitute) or 2 cloves garlic, minced
1 stalk celery, chopped
1½ tsp. salt
2 tbs. olive oil
½ cup Italian bread crumbs
Juice of 1 lemon
1 cup parmesan cheese
¼ cup parsley, chopped

Preheat oven to 350°. Scoop out insides of zucchini and set aside. In a pan, melt butter, add hing and rice. Stir for 1 minute. Add water, salt, and celery. Bring to a boil and cover, lower heat, simmer until rice is cooked (about 10 minutes). Steam the chopped insides of the zucchinis for 5 minutes. Add to the cooked rice, along with olive oil, bread crumbs, lemon juice, and parsley. Place the filling into the zucchini shells. Arrange shells in a shallow baking disk. Sprinkle with parmesan cheese and cover pan with aluminum foil. Bake for 30 minutes. Remove cover and bake another 8 minutes.

*PESTO ROSSINI
Pesto Ricotta Shells with Herbed Tomato Sauce

1½ cups fresh plum tomatoes, diced
2 tbs. olive oil
1 small onion, minced
2 medium garlic cloves, minced
1 sliced lemon
1 tbs. fresh oregano leaves
1 tbs. fresh chives, minced
1 lb. large pasta shells (jumbo)

Filling:
1 egg
1 cup ricotta cheese
½ cup parmesan, finely grated
1 cup basil pesto (see recipe)

Preheat oven to 350°. Peel and de-seed tomatoes, chop coarsely. Heat oil and sauté garlic and onion. Add tomato and lemon, simmer 15 minutes. Stir in herbs. Cook pasta shells *al dente* and rinse in cold water. To prepare *filling*, beat egg and whisk into ricotta and pesto. Stir in parmesan cheese. Put some tomato sauce in a 9x13-inch baking dish and place stuffed shells with ricotta mixture in dish. Cover with remaining sauce and bake uncovered for 20 minutes.

RISOTTO ROSSINI
Rice

5 cups vegetable or chicken stock
2 tbs. vegetable oil or butter
1 small onion, minced
1½ cup rice *(arborio)*
½ cup fresh parmesan cheese, grated

Bring the vegetable stock to a boil and simmer. Heat oil or butter in large, heavy saucepan on medium heat. Sauté onion 2-4 minutes. Add rice stir 1 minute and thoroughly coat rice with oil. Add stock. It should take about 18-20 minutes to cook the rice Remove from heat and stir. Top with grated cheese. You can serve this dish with frozen peas, or replace the parmesan with soft cheese like mascarpone or mozzarella. Add pinch of saffron, four plum tomatoes, chopped, and porchini mushrooms.

Rice Primavera

2 cups cooked rice *(arborio)*
1 orange (peeled and chopped)
1 red pepper, grated, skinned
17 oz. can corn kernels
Pineapple chunks, fresh or canned
½ cup mayonnaise
1 cup cubed cheese (Jarlsberg, Swiss, cheddar, or mozzarella)

Mix all ingredients together in bowl or pan and garnish with Spanish olives. Serve warm or chilled.

POLENTA CON FUNGHI
Cornmeal with Mushrooms

    1 cup cornmeal
    3½ cups water
    1 tsp. salt
    4 tbs. butter
    Salt and pepper
    2 tsp. olive oil
    1 lb. mushrooms, sliced (shittake optional)
    1 large garlic clove, minced
    2 tsp. fresh thyme, minced, or ½ tsp. dried

In a saucepan bring water to boil (for easier mixing, put polenta in water before boiling). Reduce heat to medium, add cornmeal and whisk. Cook for 15 minutes, stirring constantly, or until thick. Stir in butter, season with pepper. Pour *polenta* into a buttered 9″ square shallow baking pan to cook for a few minutes. Cover, chill for 30 minutes. Place *polenta* on cutting board and cut into eight squares. In skillet, heat 2 tbs. of olive oil. Add polenta squares and cook on both sides 2-3 minutes. In another saucepan, cook mushrooms, thyme, and garlic in olive oil 5-7 minutes until mushrooms are firm. Spoon over polenta and serve garnished with thyme sprigs.

*ASPARAGIALLA MILANESE
Green Asparagus with Eggs

    2–4 lbs. green asparagus (cut and trim away hard ends)
    6 eggs
    3½ oz. butter
    Salt to taste
    2½ oz. parmesan, grated
    3 tbs. extra-virgin olive oil

Quickly steam asparagus until tender; put in dish and cover with parmesan, butter, and pepper. Beat eggs, add salt and pepper; pour over asparagus. Heat oil in fry pan, add egg-asparagus mixture and cook. Gently loosen with wooden spoon. Turn omelet over and cook a few more minutes. Serve garnished with basil.

*Grandmother Grace's Eggplant Parmesan

2 or 3 medium eggplants
1 lb. fresh mozzarella
½ cup fresh parmesan and romano cheeses, grated
16-oz. Italian bread crumbs
6 eggs
4 tbs. virgin olive or vegetable oil
1 qt. marinara sauce
3 cloves garlic, minced

Peel eggplants and cut into thin round slices. Put eggplant slices in salted water (2 tsp. or more) and let sit for at least one hour. Wash and drain. (This will remove the bitterness.) Sauté garlic in oil in saucepan. Beat eggs in a bowl. Put Italian bread crumbs in a separate bowl. Dip eggplant in egg and then in bread crumbs. Lightly brown in oil. Cover bottom of casserole dish with oil and a third of the marinara sauce. Place layers of eggplant rounds, then cheeses, then eggplant, then cheeses into dish. Cover with the remaining marinara sauce and the rest of the cheese. Bake in preheated oven at 360° for 45 minutes, or until the cheese starts to bubble. Serve in stacks with fresh Italian bread.

CALZONE GABRIELLI

Dough:
2 tbs. yeast
1 cup warm water (105°)
1 tsp. salt
⅓ cup oil (not olive)
2 cups flour

Filling:
⅓ cup mozzarella, chopped
½ cup parmesan grated
1½ cups ricotta
⅓ cup parsley, chopped
1 cup deep-fried eggplant cubes
2 tsp. salt
1 tsp. pepper
¼ tsp. hing (garlic substitute) or 2 cloves minced garlic
Oil for deep frying

Add yeast to warm water and let sit for a minute. Add salt, oil, and flour. Knead for 3 minutes. Sprinkle tabletop with flour. Separate dough into 2-inch balls. Cover with damp cloth and let rise for 45 minutes. While dough is rising, mix the ingredients together. Heat oil in wok until very hot. Roll out dough balls into 6-inch circles. Divide filling into eight portions and place a portion on each round. Fold the dough over. Place fork in flour and use to seal dough edges. Fry in hot oil for 1 minute on each side, or until reddish-brown. Serve hot. (Serves 8)

*PRONTO PIZZA
Fast Pizza

    4 pita (whole wheat bread, 7-inches)
    2 cups zucchini, sliced
    1 cup black olives, sliced
    1 cup green peppers, chopped
    1½ cup fresh mozzarella, grated
    1½ cup Monterey jack cheese, grated
    ¼ cup parmesan cheese, grated
    Oregano
    Tomato sauce (see *marinara recipe*)

Preheat oven to 400°. Place two pita breads on baking sheet. Spread each with one-quarter of the tomato sauce. Top with vegetables and cheese. Sprinkle with oregano. Bake 15 minutes or until the cheese begins to bubble. Repeat with remaining pita bread.

PUCCINI ZUCCHINI
Sicilian Sweet & Sour Zucchini

    2 tbs. virgin olive oil
    1 large onion
    3 garlic cloves, chopped
    2¼ lbs. zucchini, very thinly sliced
    3 tbs. raisins or sultanas (mix golden and regular raisins)
    3 tbs. red wine vinegar
    Fresh-ground black pepper to taste

Sauté onion in olive oil until slightly golden. Add chopped garlic and stir. Add zucchini and cook, approx. 5 minutes. Add raisins, vinegar, and pepper, and cook gently for 10 minutes. While simmering, sauté 3 tbs. of pine nuts in a little butter or olive oil and add to the zucchini just before serving. Stir ingredients and mix well.

*LANZA LASAGNA
Vegie Lasagna

    3 tsp. olive oil
    ¼ lb. fresh mushrooms (1 cup thin-sliced)
    ½ cup onion, finely chopped
    ½ cup carrot, peeled and chopped
    1 garlic clove, crushed
    2 cups fresh spinach (5 oz.), packed, washed, trimmed
    ½ tsp. salt
    ⅛ tsp. fresh-ground pepper
    1 cup ricotta (see page 83)
    2 tsp. Italian flat-leaf parsley or basil, chopped
    2 tbs. parmesan cheese, grated
    2 cups fresh marinara sauce
    6 lasagna noodles, cooked and drained
    1½ cup fresh mozzarella, grated

Heat oil and sauté mushrooms, onions, and carrots. Cook 8 to 10 minutes. Add garlic and cook 1 minute. Stir in spinach and cover until wilted (3 minutes). Season with salt and pepper. Combine the ricotta cheese, purée until smooth and creamy.

  Preheat oven to 350°. In a 9x12-inch baking dish, spread ½ cup of marinara sauce on bottom. Cover with two lasagna noodles (cooked *al dente*). Spoon the spinach mixture over the pasta, and add ¼ cup of mozzarella cheese over the filing. Top with another two layers of noodles, spread ricotta over layers and repeat. Pour remaining sauce over top with the rest of the cheese. Bake 30 minutes, covered, then 20 minutes uncovered until bubbly. Let stand 15 minutes and serve.

CALAMARI ALLA GENOESE
Genoise-style Squid

3 lbs. squid (fresh or frozen)
4 tbs. oil
2 garlic cloves, minced
2 tbs. fresh parsley
1 tsp. salt
½ tsp. pepper
1 cup dry red wine
3 cups crushed tomatoes
Juice of one lemon

Clean squid and cut into squares or rings. Cut tentacles in half. Heat olive oil in a big frying pan with garlic and cook until golden brown. Add the squid, parsley, salt, and pepper. When squid starts to turn pink (3-4 minutes), pour in red wine and cook until alcohol has evaporated. Add tomatoes. Bring to a boil, lower heat to simmer, and cook for 20 minutes or until squid are tender. Add lemon juice. Serve hot with fresh Italian bread.

Broccoli Casserole

1 lb. fresh ricotta
½ cup grated cheese
4 eggs (whites only, if desired)
1 bunch of broccoli, cut long and small
2 tbs. olive oil

Lightly steam broccoli, then place in bottom of 9x13-inch baking pan on top of olive oil. Layer with ricotta cheese. Place beaten eggs on top of last layer and sprinkle with grated cheese. Bake at 450° for 20 minutes, or until done.

*CARCIOFE RIPIENI
Stuffed Artichokes

9 artichokes
1½ cups toasted Italian bread crumbs
½ cup romano cheese, grated
1 tbs. pine nuts
1 tbs. currants
1 onion
3 sprigs parsley
½ tsp. salt
½ tsp. pepper
2 tbs. olive oil

Cut artichokes in half and remove the inner leaves and the spines. Steam chokes, about 40 minutes, Until leaves are tender. Preheat oven to 375°. Mix the other ingredients in bowl and sauté in saucepan until lightly browned. Stuff into artichoke. Bake for 10 to 15 minutes.

*Stuffed Shells Sorrento

1¼ lbs. ricotta cheese
½ cup parmesan cheese
¼ tsp. nutmeg
¼ tsp. pepper
½ lb. jumbo pasta shells
½ cup fresh parsley, chopped
¼ cup fresh basil, chopped
Marinara sauce

Cook shells *al dente*. Place ricotta cheese in a bowl and mix in the rest of the ingredients. Fill the pasta shells and put into a casserole. Cover with marinara sauce and bake in a pre-heated over at 360° for 45 minutes. Serve with fresh grated parmesan.

GNOCCHI
Potato Dumplings

6 large potatoes
2 tbs. and 1 tsp. salt
Ground white pepper
2 eggs, beaten
4 cups unbleached flour
Grated parmesan

Boil potatoes about 40 minutes. Peel and dice, then set aside to cool. Bring 6 quarts of salted (2 tbs.) water to a boil.

Mound the cooled potatoes with a well in the center. Add 1 tsp. salt and dash of pepper to eggs, and pour into the well. Work the potatoes and eggs together and gradually add 3 cups of flour. Don't work the dough too long.

Place the dough on a floured work surface and cut into six parts. Continue to work dough until it no longer feels sticky. Scoop up teaspoon-sizes pieces of dough, pinching with fork, and poach them in boiling water for approximately 2 minutes. (Poach a dozen gnocchi at once.) Let drain. Serve with parmesan.

GNOCCHI DI ZUCCA
Dumplings with squash

1 butternut squash (approx. 1½ pounds)
2 eggs, beaten
1¼ tsp. salt
1½ cups flour

Cut squash in half and bake in 350° oven for half an hour. Scoop out seeds and discard. Scoop out the pulp and reserve in a bowl with whatever liquids drain from squash. Refrigerate.

Purée squash and add eggs and salt. Mix well, then add flour and blend. Dough should be soft and sticky.

Scoop up mixture in a teaspoon and poach in boiling water for 2 minutes. Drain. Serve favorite topping.

POLENTA

4 cups water
1 tbs. butter
1 bay leaf
2 tsp. salt
1½ cups yellow cornmeal (coarse)

In saucepan, bring water, butter, bay leaf, and salt to a simmer. Sift the cornmeal into mixture very slowly, stirring constantly with wire whisk. Continue stirring and cook over medium low heat. Polenta is done when smooth and thick and pulls away from the sides of the pan, about 30 minutes. Discard bay leaf and pour polenta into serving bowl and let rest for 10 minutes. (For easier mixing, put polenta in water before boiling, heat and stir constantly.)

FRIED POLENTA
Spread cooked polenta on a lightly greased pan about ¼-inch thick. Smooth surface. Refrigerate. When polenta is firm, turn out onto work surface and cut into desired shapes (squares, rectangles, triangles). Fry polenta in lightly greased skillet for approximately 10 minutes, or when lightly browned on both sides.

POLENTA CON FONDUTA DI FUNGHI PORCINI E TARTUFI
Polenta with Cheese, Mushrooms, and Truffles

½ lb. Fontina cheese
1 cup milk
2 tbs. butter, softened
2 egg yolks
1 white truffle (optional)
Salt
Fresh-ground pepper
Fried polenta (see recipe)
2 tbs. olive oil
4 cloves garlic, crushed
20 oz. porcini mushrooms
¼ cup parsley, chopped

Cut the cheese into ½-inch cubes and soak in the milk for an hour. Place in double boiler and cook, stirring, until the cheese melts and blends with milk. Add butter. Remove from heat and add egg yolks one at a time. Stir until well mixed. Shave protrusions from truffle and add to mixture. Reserve truffle. Season with salt and pepper.

Place the fried polenta in a single layer in a large flat baking dish. Top with cheese fonduta and broil until fonduta is golden.

In a large pan, sautée garlic and mushrooms in olive oil until brown. Discard garlic and dry mushrooms on paper towel. Sprinkle with parsley and serve with the fonduta-topped polenta. Shave the reserved truffle over the fonduta at the table.

Homemade Rossini Ricotta Cheese

1 gallon milk
1 qt. buttermilk

In a 3-4 gallon pot, bring milk to a boil. When it begins to rise, lower the heat. While stirring with a wooden spoon, slowly add the buttermilk. Let curdle for about one minute. Cut just enough cheesecloth to place over the top of a 2-gallon bowl or pot. Secure the cheesecloth with rubber bands or tie with a string so it doesn't slip into bowl. Pour liquid into cheesecloth very slowly. The cheese will stay on top and the whey (clear yellowish liquid) will go to the bottom. To get the maximum amount of cheese, bring the whey liquid to a boil again and pour through cheesecloth. Continue process until the whey is almost clear. Remove cheesecloth with the ricotta and twist into a small ball-shape. Place in bowl and refrigerate overnight. Place whey in another container and refrigerate.

Next day: Take ricotta from cheesecloth and put in bowl. Stir in whey to get desired consistency (more whey for a creamier texture). Use a fork to press ricotta into a softer texture. Use ricotta in lasagna, cannolis, stuffed shells, and more.

Drink the whey. It's good for you. (1 cup whey=64 calories, 2.2 g protein, 0.7 g fat, 12.5 g carbohydrates, 125 mg calcium, 130 mg phosophorus, 0.2 mg iron, 20 IUs of Vitamin A; no sodium, or potassium.

La Dolce Vita

I KNOW WHAT YOU'RE THINKING—sweets = calories! Okay, but you can eat them in moderation and adjust the recipes to fit your diet . . . or you can just go for it!

Sweets are very grounding. They have lots of the element of earth in them, and some of us need to be in more touch with the earth—or grounded. Catch my drift?

Many celebrations at our house had an abundance of sweets to balance the rest of the flavors—salty, sour, pungent, bitter, and astringent. I find it hard to pass up some mouth-watering desserts; to deny myself would create more stress, so I just indulge with moderation. Sometimes I'll go into an Italian restaurant and order just a dessert and a cup of decaf cappuccino and be in bliss. It's worrying about too many calories that creates more fat cells. Know what I mean? Don't deny yourself anything in this life that is fun—and desserts are fun. They keep us in mind of celebrations, good times, laughter, and good friends. "Good desserts always make good friends, and good friends always make good desserts."

You may have tried some of the following desserts, either at home or from a bakery. When they're made fresh they'll be the hit of the meal or the season. Some of these recipes are made only around the holidays in our family, but you can make them any time the occasion arises. These desserts will make anybody sing!

*Nut Bars

2½ cups flour
2 eggs
1 tbs grated lemon rind
1½ cups sugar
1 tsp. rum extract
1 tsp. anise extract or 2 tsp. anisette
⅓ cup milk
1 cup slivered almonds
1 cup whole hazelnuts or halved brazil nuts
2 tsp. baking powder

In a large bowl, combine all the ingredients except the nuts. Beat until well blended. Add nuts and mix well. Divide in half and shape into a long roll. Place both rolls on a well-greased sheet and bake at 350°F for 25-30 minutes or until light brown. Remove from oven and cool 10-15 minutes or until easy to slice. Cut into cross-wise slices and place cut side down on sheet. Return to oven to toast slightly (10 minutes). Remove from oven and cover with dish towel for 10 minutes.

*Chocolate Cookies

> 5 cups flour
> 1 cup sugar
> 1½ tsp. baking powder
> 3 tbs. cocoa
> ½ cup margarine
> 1 cup milk
> 1½ tsp. allspice
> 1½ tsp cinnamon
> 1 tsp. nutmeg
> 1 cup chopped walnuts

Reserve one cup of flour. Sift remaining dry ingredients together. Add margarine to mixture and combine, as for pie crust. Add milk and nuts. Knead in enough of the reserved flour to make a soft dough. Pinch off pieces of dough the size of a walnut and roll into a ball. Place on a greased cookie sheet and bake at 350° for 10-12 minutes. Cool.

Frosting:
> 2½ cups 10x (extra-fine) sugar
> 1-2 tbs. orange juice
> 1 tbs. margarine
> Milk, as needed

Combine all ingredients and add milk to make medium-thick consistency. Roll cookies in frosting. Let cool and serve.

Sesame Seed Cookies

>3 eggs
>1½ cups shortening
>1½ cups sugar
>1½ tsp. baking powder
>½ cup milk, plus milk for dipping
>2½ cups flour
>1 tsp. vanilla
>4 oz. sesame seeds

Combine the dry ingredients, except for the seeds. Add shortening as for a pie crust. Add eggs, milk and vanilla. Shape into logs, half-inch thick. Cut into 1½ inch lengths and dip into milk, then into seeds.Place on greased cookie sheet and bake at 375°F for 10-12 minutes or until browned.

Sicilian Almond Cookies (Grandma's "S" Cookies)

>1 cup honey
>1 lb. almonds (roasted and ground)
>2 tbs. cinnamon
>6 cups flour (use 3 cups flour for smaller yield)
>1½ cups sugar
>6 tsp. baking powder
>2½ sticks margarine, melted
>4 eggs
>½ cup milk
>1 tsp. vanilla

Bring honey to a boil, add almonds and cinnamon, mix well and cool. Make well in flour and add the rest of the ingredients (more flour if needed), mix and knead dough well. Roll out and make strips about ¾-inch wide and 6 inches long (or longer). Almond mixture should be firm. Take a small amount and roll to fit on half of the strip of dough. Fold over and twist to shape of an "S." Bake 12 minutes at 375°.

*TIRAMI-SU
Pick Me Up
Casserole-dish size:
1 lb. fresh mascarpone cheese
¼ cup extra-fine sugar
2 tbs. light rum
2 dozen champagne biscuits
1 cup espresso, freshly brewed
1 6-egg Zabaglione recipe (see page 111)
2 tbs. unsweetened cocoa powder

In a food processor with plastic blade, mix in the mascarpone, sugar, and rum until smooth (about 3 pulses). Arrange 6 biscuits side by side on a plate. Moisten with a third of the espresso (put espresso in hand-sprayer and spray on lady fingers). Spread a third of the cheese mixture over the biscuits. Repeat twice each, and finish with the cheese mixture. Cut remaining biscuits in half lengthwise.

Make the six-egg batch of Zabaglione (6 egg yolks, 6 tbs. sugar, 12 tbs. Marsala) and pour over top of the dessert. Press 12 biscuit halves into the Zabaglione to make a fence around the layers. Sprinkle with cocoa.

Dessert-bowl size:
1 dozen Lady Fingers
8 egg whites
½ lb. sugar
6 oz. mascarpone cheese
6 oz. whipped cream
4 oz. dark chocolate
1 cup cold espresso

Whisk egg whites and mascarpone cheese in bowl until smooth. Add sugar and whipped cream (rum optional). Dip Lady Fingers in espresso and arrange along sides of small dessert bowl. Put cream in middle and press down Lady Fingers on top. Turn over on plate and pour chocolate over. Refrigerate for 10 minutes. Garnish with mint or fresh fruit.

*Ricotta Cake

6 eggs, well beaten
3 lbs. ricotta (see page 88)
1 cup sugar
½ cup flour
2 tsp. vanilla
½ cup chocolate chips (optional)

In a bowl, beat eggs well. Drain water from ricotta, then fold into eggs, along with sugar, flour, vanilla, and chocolate chips. Butter bottom of 9-inch spring-form pan and coat with flour or graham cracker crumbs. Bake in 375° oven for 1 hour. Cool in oven. Serve with fresh cherries, fruit, or powdered sugar.

Ricotta Puffs

3 eggs
1 lb. ricotta (see page 88)
3 tbs. sugar
4 tsp. baking powder
1 cup flour
½ tsp. salt
1 tsp. vanilla
Vegetable oil

Beat eggs in a bowl until fluffy. Stir in cheese. Add other ingredients and mix well. Let dough stand for one hour. Fill sauce pan with at least ½-inch oil, enough to cover puffs. Heat oil to 350°. Using a tablespoon, drop mixture into oil and fry for 3 minutes or until golden brown. Drain on paper towel, and sprinkle with powdered sugar

*BISCOTTI BAMBINI
Twice-baked Cookies

    3 tbs. butter or margarine (soft)
    ⅔ cup sugar
    2 eggs
    ½ tsp. almond extract
    1½ cup flour
    ½ cup unsweetened cocoa
    1½ tsp. baking powder
    ½ tsp. baking soda
    ½ cup coarsely chopped almonds or 1 cup ground hazelnuts

Beat the eggs, butter, sugar, almond extract together. Combine flour and rest of ingredients into the mixture. With floured hands, mix dough and break into two 12-inch loafs. Preheat oven to 350° and put each section on a 10x15-inch cookie sheet. Cut each section into six or eight long pieces and bake for 20 minutes. Take out of oven and let cool. Add toppings, if any, and bake again for another 20

*CREMA CAROMELLA
Baked Custard

2 cups milk, or ½ milk and ½ heavy cream
1 whole egg
3 egg yolks
½ tsp. vanilla
¼ cup sugar
¼ tsp. lemon rind

Topping:
⅔ cup sugar
4 tbs. water

Have a warm oven-proof dish ready. Blend the milk, eggs, vanilla, sugar, and lemon rind. In a small saucepan, slowly stir ⅔ cup sugar and water over medium low heat until the sugar turns golden brown. Pour into the baking dish. Make sure the caramel is evenly distributed on the sides and the bottom. Pour in the milk mixture. Place custard-filled dish in oven and bake at 300° for 1¼ hour. It should look like gelatin when ready.

Italian Sesame Cookies

1¼ lb. flour (4 cups)
¾ lb. confectioner's sugar
3 tbs. baking powder
1 lb. butter (at room temp.)
3 tbs. vanilla
6 eggs
1½ lbs. sesame seeds

Mix flour, sugar, and baking powder. Cut in butter until blended. Add 3 eggs and vanilla. Knead together until smooth. Break off small amount of dough and roll with palms of the hand into long roll-shape, about 2½ inches long. Beat remaining 3 eggs. Dip the shaped cookie into egg and roll in sesame seeds. Place on cookie sheet and bake at 400° oven until golden.

Italian Easter Cookies

3-6 eggs
¼ lb. butter
1 cup sugar
3 cups flour
Juice of 1 orange
1 tbs. melted butter
Confectioners sugar
3 tsp. baking powder
Salt
1 tsp. vanilla, almond, or anise extract

Beat the eggs well. Gradually add sugar, then melted butter, vanilla and orange juice. Fold in flour, baking powder, and salt. Form dough into a rectangle and shape about 8x3. Bake at 375° oven about 25-30 minutes. When cooled, frost and slice about 1 inch wide. You can also drop the cookies onto a cookie sheet.

Anise Cookies

¾ cup butter
1 cup sugar
4 eggs
4 cups flour
3 tbs. baking powder
1 tsp. anise seeds
1 cup pecans or almonds (chopped)
1 cup milk, plus milk for brushing
Pinch of salt

Cream the butter and sugar until light. Add eggs one at a time until fluffy, then add milk. Combine flour, baking powder, salt, and seeds, then mix into cream mixture and stir in nuts. Divide into quarters. Place on oiled cookie sheet. With floured hands, form four rolls 1½ inch wide to the length of the cookie sheet. Bake for 30 to 35 minutes in a 350° oven, then cut diagonally into ¾ inch slices. Brush with milk and sprinkle with sugar or honey. Return to oven and bake 10 minutes more, until toasted and crisp.

No-Bake Rum Cake

2 packages anisette sponge cookies
¼ cup rum, mixed with ¾ cup of water (filtered)
2 3-oz.packages of chocolate and vanilla pudding (not instant)
8 oz. fresh whipped cream

Using a spring mold pan, layer 1 package of cookies on their sides, covering the bottom of pan. Sprinkle with half the rum-water mixture. Pour warm cooked pudding over cookies and the rest of the liquid, then the rest of the pudding. Refrigerate for at least one day. When ready, spread with whipped cream. You can also add chopped walnuts.

STRUFOLI

4 cups flour
4 tsp. baking powder
1 cup sugar
½ cup butter
3 eggs (whites, if so desired)
2 tsp. vanilla
Pinch of salt
Honey, warmed

Mix butter with flour mixture. Make a hole in flour and add eggs, salt, vanilla. Then knead, adding a little flour at a time. Roll in strips, cut in bite-size pieces and fry in vegetable oil until golden brown. Drain in brown paper bag and put Strufoli in hot honey.

Mamma's Easter Papoose Bread

¼ cup luke-warm water
½ cup plus 1 tsp. sugar
1 package active dry yeast
1 cup scalded milk
Salt
⅓ cup butter
2 eggs beaten
3½ cups flour
1 egg (beaten well with a tsp. water)
6 eggs, hard-boiled
Confetti sprinkles

Combine the water, 1 tsp. sugar, and yeast in a small bowl. Let stand for 5 minutes. In a large bowl, combine the milk, salt, butter, eggs, and remaining ½ cup of sugar. Add about half the flour and beat until smooth. Stir in the yeast mixture. Slowly add remaining flour to form a stiff dough. Knead until smooth. Place in an oiled bowl and let rise till double. Punch dough and divide in six pieces. Roll pieces into a 1-inch thick roll and make a v-shape. Place an egg on the inside of each v, twist the length forming a fishtail at the bottom. Brush with egg mixture, sprinkle with confetti, place on oiled sheet, and bake at 350° for 35 minutes.

*Summer Dolce

    2 ripe mangos, peeled and sliced
    3 peaches, peeled and sliced
    1 ripe cantaloupe (scooped out with small ball scoop)
    2 small baskets of fresh strawberries (frozen if fresh not
        available)
    4 bananas
    1 medium papaya
    Coconut shavings

Prepare all the fruit in a large bowl. Cube the papaya, and slice the bananas in large angular cuts. Let chill in the refrigerator. Serve with shaved coconut.

Fall Dolce

    2 Anjou or Bosc pears
    3 apples (Granny Smith or Pippin)
    8 oz. fresh or dried figs (12)
    ½ cup raisins

Cook the pears and apples in water with some apple juice for about 5 or 6 minutes or until tender. Add the figs and raisins. Drain from water and serve with Almond Biscotti.

Italian Pineapple Ice with Raspberry Kirsch

2 cups fresh pineapple, chopped and cored, or 16-oz. can
crushed pineapple
2 cups water
½ cup sugar
¼ cup lemon juice
Raspberry kirsch

Bring water and sugar to a boil in a heavy saucepan, approximately 5 minutes, stirring until sugar is dissolved. Remove from heat and stir in pineapple and lemon juice. Cool and pour into a shallow bowl. Put in freezer for 30 minutes. Stir vigorously and return to freezer. When half frozen, mix with electric mixer on medium speed for 1 minute, then freeze until firm. Put in small dessert dishes or glasses and pour raspberry kirsch over the them.

Avocado Lemon-Lime Pie

1 cup avocado, puréed
1 can sweetened condensed milk
1 tsp. grated lemon and lime rind
½ cup lime juice (key lime juice in bottle is fine)
2 egg yolks
1 pre-baked 9-inch pastry shell

Mix the milk, rinds, juice, egg yolks, and a dash of salt in a bowl. Stir until thickened. Fold in puréed avocado and pour into shell. Chill for 2 hours. Garnish with lime slices and fresh mint leaves.

*SFOGLIATELLE NAPOLETANÈ

Pastry:
    2 cups flour
    1½ cups butter/margarine
    2 tbs. sugar
    2 eggs
    Milk
    Salt

Filling:
    1 whole egg
    3 egg yolks
    ½ cup super-fine sugar
    1 tbs. cornstarch
    1¼ cup hot milk
    1 egg (beaten)
    ½ tbs. vanilla extract
    ½ cup ricotta cheese
    2 tbs. diced orange or lemon peel
    Powdered sugar

Combine the flour, butter, sugar, eggs, and salt. Add milk to give dough a soft elastic consistency. Knead well, cover, and chill for 30-40 minutes.

To make the filling, beat 1 egg and 3 yolks with the sugar and add cornstarch. Slowly add milk and vanilla, then pour into pan. Place on low heat. Bring to a boil, stirring constantly. Remove from heat and let cool. Mix ricotta and orange peel. Preheat oven to 375°. Roll out pastry on floured board and cut into rectangles. Put filling on half of the rectangles and cover with remaining rectangles. Seal edges firmly. Brush with beaten egg. Arrange on greased, floured baking sheet and bake until golden brown. Dust with powdered sugar.

*Neapolitan Cheesecake

Use an 8-inch spring-form pan. Preheat oven to 350°

Crust:
　　⅓ cup ground walnuts
　　1½ tsp. melted butter
　　2 tbs. Turbinado sugar
　　¼ cup flour
　　2 tsb. water

Combine the ingredients and press onto bottom of buttered spring-form pan.

Bottom layer (chocolate or carob):
　　4 tsp. chocolate powder
　　⅓ cup whipping cream
　　½ cup sour cream
　　12 oz. cream cheese (softened)
　　½ cup Turbinado sugar
　　1 tsp. cornstarch

Blend all the ingredients in blender until smooth. Pour on top of crust.

Middle layer (vanilla):
　　1½ tsp. vanilla
　　⅓ cup whipping cream
　　½ cup sour cream
　　12 oz. cream cheese (softened)
　　½ cup Turbinado sugar
　　1 tsp. cornstarch

Blend all ingredients in a blender until smooth. Pour gently over the chocolate layer.

Top layer (Strawberry):
   3 tbs. strawberry jam (strawberries and sugar)
   ½ cup whipping cream
   ½ cup sour cream
   12 oz. cream cheese (softened)
   ½ cup Turbinado sugar
   1 tsp. cornstarch

Blend all ingredients in blender until smooth. Pour gently over the vanilla layer. Bake in oven for 50 minutes. Let stand on cooling rack for 30 minutes, then refrigerate for at least 3 hours. Serve cool. (Serves 12)

Italian Lemon Sherbet

   1 cup whipping cream
   1 cup yogurt (plain)
   ⅔ cup sugar
   Juice from 1 lemon
   1½ tsp. grated lemon peel

In a bowl, combine whipping cream and sugar. Whip with mixer on high speed. Fold in lemon juice, yogurt, and lemon peel. Put in freezer. Stir every 45 minutes, until frozen (about 5 hours).

CROSTATA
Fruit tart shell

4½ cups flour
1½ cups sugar
2 tsp. baking powder
Salt
3 eggs, beaten
¾ lb. butter, softened
¼ tsp. almond extract
(enough for three pies)

Combine flour, sugar, baking powder, and salt in a large bowl. Add eggs and stir or mix with hands until crumbly. Work in the butter and almond extract until butter is no longer visible. Divide dough into three portions and shape each into a ball, then flatten into thick disks. Wrap each piece separately in plastic wrap and refrigerate until firm.

Roll out dough on floured surface to ⅛-inch thick. (If dough is too cold to work, let soften slightly.) Transfer the rolled-out dough to a 10-inch tart pan (with a removable bottom). Prick the dough on the bottom with a fork and trim off excess overhang. Freeze for only 10 minutes. Bake shell 30 minutes at 350°.

CROSTATA DI MELE ALLA CREME
Apple-Custard Tart

1 unbaked tart shell (10-inch)
2 med. tart apples
2 eggs
¼ cup sugar
⅔ cup heavy cream
½ tsp. vanilla extract
¼ cup apricot jam (smooth)
3 tbs. hot water

Bake shell in 350° oven for 15 minutes. Remove and cool.

Peel and core apples; slice each into 16 wedges. Beat eggs and sugar together. Add cream and vanilla extract; mix well until sugar is dissolved.

Spread 2 tbs. of apricot jam inside tart shell and arrange apple slices on top of jam. Transfer tart to baking sheet and pour custard mixture over apples. Bake about 40 minutes at 350°.

Cool tart on a rack. Melt remaining apricot jam in 3 tbs. of hot water. Brush the mixture over the surface of the tart and serve at room temperature or slightly cooled.

CANNOLI E SICILIANI

SHELLS
1¾ cups unsifted flour
½ tsp. salt
2 tbs. sugar
1 egg slightly beaten
2 tbs. firm butter cut into pieces
¼ cup dry Sauterne
1 egg white, slightly beaten
1-2 cups extra-virgin olive oil for deepy frying

FILLING
(Fills 1 dozen or more regular cannolis or 3 dozen bite-size)
1½ lbs. fresh-made ricotta cheese (see page 88)
½ cup confectioners sugar
¼ tsp. cinnamon
½ square bittersweet chocolate, grated, or chocolate chips
3 capfuls vanilla extract
3 tbs. chopped citron (optional)
3 tbs. chopped candied orange peel
6 glacé cherries, cut up
¼ cup orange juice (optional)

SHELLS
Sift flour with salt and sugar. Make a well in the center and place egg and butter in it. Stir with fork from center out to moisten flour mixture. Add sauterne wine a tablespoon at a time until dough forms ball or clings together. Cover and let stand for 15 minutes.

Roll out dough on floured board to about 1/16-of an inch thick. Cut into 3½-inch circles. With rolling pin, roll circles into ovals. Wrap around forms or wooden dowels and seal edges with egg white. Turn out ends of dough to flare slightly. Fry in very hot oil, two or three at a time, at 350° for 1 minute or until lightly brown. Remove and drain on paper towel. Cool for 5 seconds then slip from form. Cool completely before filling.

FILLING

Mix fresh ricotta with all ingredients in large bowl until creamy. In a piping (pastry) bag or with spoon, fill shells shortly before serving so that they maintain their crispness. After filing, ends may be dipped in finely chopped pistachio nuts or shaved chocolate.

Chocolate Zabaglione Sauce

6 egg yolks
¼ cup dry Marsala
¼ cup sugar
3 oz. semi-sweet chocolate, chopped and melted

In a double boiler, whisk together the egg yolks, Marsala, and sugar until fluffy, light, and hot (3–4 minutes). Remove from heat and slowly fold in the melted chocolate. Spoon sauce over Tirami-Su while hot.

GRANITA DI PESCA
Peach Granita

2 cups water
1 lb. unpeeled ripe peaches or ripe mangos
⅓ cup sugar
2 tbs. fresh lemon juice
1 drop vanilla extract
Mint leaves (garnish)

Bring water to a boil in medium saucepan. Add peaches and sugar and simmer gently 30 minutes. Cool peaches in the liquid, then strain the mixture through a sieve, maintaining as much pulp as possible. Add lemon juice and vanilla extract. Freeze 45 minutes to 1 hour, scraping the ice crystals that form around the edges into the center every ten minutes. Mixture should be even, with a grainy consistency. Scoop granita into chilled serving glasses and garnish with mint leaves.

GRANITA DI CAFFÈ
Coffee Granita

½ cup sugar
1 cup water
2 cups strong espresso, cooled
½ pint heavy cream, whipped with 1 tbs. sugar
Chocolate-covered coffee beans for garnish

Combine sugar and water in a saucepan, bring to a simmer, and cook 5 minutes. Let cool, then add espresso and stir well. Pour into a 9x13-inch metal baking pan and freeze. Stir every 8-10 minutes to break up the ice crystals that form along edges. Should take about an hour. Scoop the granita into chilled serving glasses and top with whipped cream and garnish with chocolate-covered coffee beans.

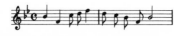

The Song Lyrics

Arrivederci, Roma

Lyrics by C. Sigman, music by R. Rascel

Arrivederci, Roma
Goodbye, goodbye to Rome.
City of a million moonlit places
City of a million warm embraces.
Where I found the one
Of all the faces far from home.
Arrivederci, Roma.
It's time for us to part.
Save the wedding bells for my returning,
Keep my lover's arms outstretched and yearning,
Please be sure the flame of love
Keeps burning in her/his heart.

Funiculì-Funiculà

L. Denza (English: H. Johnson)

Stasera, Nina mia,
io son montato
Te lo dirò? Te lo dirò?
Colà dove dispeti
un cor ingrato
Più far non può, più far non può.
Colà cocente è il foco,
ma se fuggi
Ti lascia star, ti lascia star.
E non ti corre appresso,
e non ti struggi
A riguardar, Ariguardar

Lesti, Lesti, via, montiam su là
Lesi, lesti, via montiam su là
Funiculì, funiculà, funiculì, funiculà!
Via montiam su là,
funiculì funiculà

Funiculì-Funiculà

Oh why should any heart
be filled with sadness
We should be gay, we should be gay.
Oh my, the world should
all be filled with gladness,
in ev'ry way, in ev'ry way.
A song can make most anybody happy,
so let us sing, yes, let us sing.
My song is full of life
and good and snappy
It's got the swing, and ev'ry thing.
Join the chorus, now's the time to start
Sing the chorus with a happy heart
Funiculì, funiculà, funiculì, funiculà!
Let the echo ring and sing it
With a happy heart.

Torna a Sorrento

Lyrics by G.B. DeCurtis, music by E. DeCurtis

Guardail mare come bello,
Spira tanto sentimento,
Come il tuo soave accento che me
Desto fasognar,
Senti come lieve sale,
Dai giardiniodar dàranci:
Un profumo accossi Fino,
Dinto o core se ne va,
E tu dici lo parto, addio!
Tallontani dal mio core,
Questa terra dell amore
Hai la forza di la sciai?
Ma non mi fuggir,
Non darmi piu tormento
Tor na a Sorrento, famme campa

Return to Sorrento

O'er the sea and sunlight dancing,
Waking thoughts of tender feeling,
I have seen your eyes reflecting
This same light that makes me dream.
When I pass a lovely garden,
Breathing scent of many blossoms;
There's a memory and a picture
Of but you within my heart.
Now you say goodbye, I'm leaving,
This poor heart of mine is grieving,
Can it be that you've forgotten
Can it be that love is gone?
Say not farewell, and leave a heart's that's
     broken,
Come back to Sorrento, that I may live.

Santa Lucia

Lyrics by D. Savino

Sul mare luccica
L'astro d'argento,
Placi da è l'onda,
Prospero è il ventò;
Sul mare luccica
L'astro d'argento,
Placida è l'onda,
Prospero è il ventò;
Venite all'agile
Barchetta mia
Santa Lucia!
Santa Lucia!
Venite all'agile
Barchetta mia
Santa Lucia
Santa Lucia!

Here in the Twilight

Twilight is drawing near,
Bright stars will soon appear.
Come out and meet me dear,
I want you badly.
Each star that's in the sky,
Twinkles for you and I
Don't leave me here to sigh,
I love you madly.
Santa Lucia,
Santa Lucia.
I can see your loving eyes so bright,
Just like the starlight.
Santa Lucia
Santa Lucia,
Whisper that you will be mine tonight
Here in the twilight.

Non Ti Scorda Di Me

De Curtis, Furno

Partirono le rondini dal mio paese fredo e senza
    sole
Cercando primavere di viole
Nidi'd amore e di felicita
La mia picola rondine parti
Senza laciami un bacio
Senza un addio parti.
Non ti scordar di me
La vita mia legata èa te.
Io t'amo sempre più
Nel sogno mio rimani tu.
Non ti scorda di me
La vita mia legata èa te
C'è sempre un nido nel mio cor per te
Non ti scorda di me.

Do Not Forget Me

The swallows leave from my home
     town,
My cold town without sun,
Looking for a spring of violets,
Nests of love and happiness.
My little swallot left,
Without leaving me a kiss,
Without a goodbye.
Do not forget me
My life is tied to you,
I love you forever more,
In my dreams you remain.
Do not forget me,
My life is tied to you,
There is always a nest in my heart for
     you,
Do not forget me.

M'appari tut'amor
Friedrich von Flotow

M'appari tut'amor,
il mio sguardo l'incontrò;
Bella si che il mio cor,
Ansioso a lei volò;
me feri, m'invaghi
Quell'angelica beltà,
sculta in cor dall'amor
Cancellarsi no potra,
Il pensier di poter
Palpitar con lei d'amor,
Può sopir il martir,
Che m'affanna e strazia il cor,
e strazzia il cor.

M'appari tut'amor,
il mio sguardo l'incontrò;
Bella si che il mio cor,
Ansioso a lei volò;
Marta, Marta, tu sparisti,
E il mio cor col tuo m'ardò!
Tu la pace mi rapisti,
Di dolor io morirò.
Ah, do dolor morrò, si, morrò!

None So Fair

None so rare, none so fair,
Yet enraptured mortal heart;
Maiden dear, past compare,
Ah 'twas death from thee to part!
Ere I saw thy sweet face,
On my heart there was no mace
Of that love from above
That in sorrow now I prove,
But alas! Thou art gone,
And in grief I mourn alone;
Life a shadow doth seem,
And my joy a fleeting dream,
a fleeting dream!

None so rare, none so fair,
Yet enraptured mortal heart;
Maiden dear, past compare,
Ah, 'twas death for thee to part!
Martha, Martha! I conjure thee
Leave me not to lone despair!
Let me grieve not, I implore thee,
Or return, my life to share.
Oh, come, my life to share, Ah! Return!

La Donna è Mobile

Giuseppe Verdi

La donna è mobile qual piuma al vento,
Muta d'accento e di pensiero.
Sempre un a mabile leggiadro viso,
In pianto o in riso è menzognero.
La donna è mobile, qual piuma la vento,
Muta d'accento e di pensier.
E di pensier, e di pensier.

È sempre misero chi a lei s'affida,
Chi le confida, malcauto il core!
Pur mai non sentesi, felice appieno
Chi su quel seno non liba a more!
La donna è mobile, qual piuma al vento,
Muta d'accento e di pensier.
E di pensier, e di pensier.

Woman is Fickle

Woman is fickle, false altogether;
Moves like a feather borne on the breezes.
Women with witching smile, will e'er deceive
  you.
Often will grieve you, yet, as she pleases;
Her heart's unfeeling, false altogether;
Moves like a feather borne on the breeze.
Borne on the breeze. Ah! Borne on the breeze.

Wretched the day is, when she looks kindly,
Trusts to her blindly his life thus wasting.
Yet he must surely be, dull beyond measure;
Who of love's happiness, ne'er has been tasting.
Woman is unfeeling, false altogether;
Moves like a feather borne on the breeze.
Borne on the breeze. Ah! Borne on the breeze!

Volare, Nel Blu, Dipinto Di Blu

Migliacci D. Modugno

Penso che un sogno così non ritorni mai più,
Mi dipingevo le mani e la faccia di blu,
Poi d'improviso venivo dal vento rapito
E incominciavo a volare nel cielo infinito.

Volare, oh, oh! Cantare, oh, oh, oh, oh!
Nel blu, dipinto di blu
Felice di stare lassù.
E volavo, volavo felice più in alto
Del sole ed ancora più su,
Mentre il mondo pian piano spariva lontano
   laggiù,
Una musica dolce suonava soltanto per me.
Volare, oh, oh! Cantare, oh, oh, oh, oh!
Nel blu, dipinto di blu,
Felice di stare lassù
Nel blu, dipinto di blu,
Felice di stare lassù

Volare, Let's Fly Away to the Clouds

Sometimes the world is a valley of heartaches and
    tears,
And in the hustle and bustle, no sunshine appears.
But you and I have our love always there to remind
    us,
There is a way we can leave all the shadows behind
    us.

Volare, oh, oh! Cantare, oh, oh, oh, oh!
Let's fly way up to the clouds,
Away from the mad'ning crowds.
We can sing in the glow of a star that I know of,
Where lovers enjoy peace of mind,
Let us leave the confusion and all disillusion behind,
Just like the birds of a feather
A rainbow together we'll find.
Volare, oh, oh! Cantare, oh, oh, oh, oh!
No wonder my happy heart sings,
Your love has given me wings.

O Sole Mio

Teschemacher, Di-Capua

La la la la la . . .
Che bella cosa na iurnata e sole,
Naria serena doppo na tempesta!
Pell aria fresca pare gia na festa,
Che bella cosa na iurna ta e sole.
Ma na tu sole, chiu bello, ohine,
O Sole Mio, stanfronte a te
O sole, O sole mio
Stanfronte a te, stan fronte a te.
La la la la la . . .
Quanno fa notte O sole se ne scenne
Me vene qua see na malincunia
Sotto a fenesta toia restaria
Quanno fa notte O sole se ne scenne
Man na tu sole, chiu bello, ohine,
O Sole Mio, stanfronte a te
O sole, O sole mio
Stanfronte a te, stan fronte a te.

O Sole Mio

What sheer delight is a day of sunshine
A clear blue sky when the storm is over!
The very freshness brings a festive feeling!
What sheer delight is a day of sunshine!
Another sunshine, with brighter rays,
Is shed upon me, from your dear face.
The sun, the sun that warms me,
Is in your face, is in your face.
When twilight's falling and the sun is setting.
A sense of sorrow pervades my being.
Beneath your window, would I tarry
 dreaming,
When twilight's falling, and the sun is
 setting.

That's Amore

Lyrics by Jack Brooks, music by Harry Warren

In Napoli, where love is king,
Where boy meets girl, here's what they sing:
When the moon hits your eye
Like a big pizza pie
That's amore.
When the world seems to shine
Like you've had too much wine
That's amore.
Bells will ring, ting-a-ling-a-ling,
   ting-a-ling-a-ling,
And you'll sing Veeta Bella.
Hearts will play, tippy tippy tay,
   tippy tippy tay,
Like a gay tarantella.
When the stars make you drool
Just like pasta fazool,
That's amore.
When you walk down the street
With a cloud at your feet,
You're in love
When you walk in dream,
But you know you're not dreaming, Signore,
Scuzza me, but you see,
Back in old Napoli,
That's amore!

Inspirational Sources

ITALY IS THE LAND OF SONG! Almost everywhere one goes throughout the countryside, there's a melody that's playing in someone's heart. The patron saint of music is St. Cecilia. I wonder what her favorite pasta dish was.

A person who sings is a happy person. Singing allows us to open our hearts and communicate our deep emotions to the world through song. Melodies that please the ears—as yes!—those beautiful notes from a voice as smooth as silver that sends shivers up and down one's spine. That's what happens to me when I sing and when I hear some of the great singers. *Canzone* means "song" in Italian. A song of life.

I wanted to dedicate this chapter to some of the great classical singers, Italian and Swedish, who have moved peoples' hearts and souls through singing. Immortal is the way to describe them. I hope you enjoy reading about them. Maybe you will be inspired to get some of their recordings, and sing along with them while you cook.

I keep a pitch pipe in my car (a c-to-c pitch) so I can tune up just about everywhere I go and sing to my heart's content. The next best thing to having a piano in your pocket, a pitch pipe is very portable.

Don't be afraid to open your lungs and sing out. It doesn't matter how it sounds or what anyone has told you in the past about the quality of your voice. Just do it for yourself. It's very magical and healing, and you'll enjoy it. Maybe you'll be delightfully surprised by what comes out of you.

People tell me they sing only in the shower. If that's what it takes to get one to sing, then pretend you're in the shower while you're cooking, and go for it!

Make every note count. Each breath breathes life into the notes, so give each and every note its full breath of life. Sing! Sing as if you were caressing every note!

The Grand Dame of Voice

"The teachers of men drink their life from pure sources, and take their message more directly from the soul of existence."
(Powell, 1925)

It was like a miracle meeting her. I had made a silent commitment to myself not to hide my talent for singing anymore. I wanted to manifest a teacher who had all the qualities I desired and needed. He or she had to be able to teach me to sing in Italian and, at the same time, to understand it. I grew up with the traditional Neapolitan songs, but never really understood them. My teacher would need a lot of patience and, of course, be within my budget.

Giovanna d'Onofrio, eighty-nine years young, was born in a little town in Pennsylvania and was world-traveled. She had studied in Rome. Her great uncle was a bishop and helped her take courses at a private school, though she never officially enrolled. I was introduced to her through a student of hers whom I met while getting a chiropractic adjustment. Right place, right time! Her family knew all the great singers in their heyday: Enrico Caruso, Beniamino Gigli, Eva Tetrazzini, and Mario Lanza. She traveled with some of them and picked up tips and age-old secrets. She had been through both world wars and knew a couple of popes and the world's wealthiest. The Hollywood studios hired her in the 1950-60s to heal and train some of the great voices. She was billed as a "voice constructionist."

D'Onofrio saved many voices that almost went under the surgeon's knife for polyps and sores. She knew that most singers just needed rest and instruction in breathing and how to use the full body.

"The arias of the eighteenth century are seldom focused on anymore, for there are few singers who can do them justice," she said. According to her, there were too few teachers left who could teach. She is definitely a dying breed.

"It's the vowels that sing in Italian," she once said. "The consonants are like a tennis racket: they propel forth the vowels into space. One cannot hold onto music, for it is not of this world. Once it is played or sung, it travels to another dimension."

"Excitement and Italian are one word." Giovanna d'Onofrio

Andy Lo Russo

BENIAMINO GIGLI

(Born in Recanati, Italy, March 20, 1890; died in Rome, November 30, 1957)

An Italian tenor whose father was a shoemaker, Gigli started singing in the church choir at the age of seven. His teachers were Cotogni and Rosati. He won an international competition in 1914 and made a successful debut in *La Gioconda* at Rovigo, Italy. Gigli sang in many countries, but the highlight of his career was his brilliant debut in *Mephistofele* at the Metropolitan Opera, where he remained the principal tenor for twelve consecutive seasons. He sang no fewer than twenty-eight of his sixty roles at the Met. Smoothness, sweetness, and fluency were the outstanding marks of Gigli's singing. Such perfection as he offered in his own style is not to be expected more than once in a generation. Gigli was something less than a great artist, but as a singer he was among the greatest.

ENRICO CARUSO

(Born in Naples, February 27, 1873; died in Naples, August 1, 1921)

Italian-born of poor parents, Caruso first sang as a child in churches. He studied with Guglielmo Vergine and made his debut on November 16, 1894, in Morelli's *L'amico Francesco* at the Teatro Nuovo in Naples. The exceptional appeal of his voice was, in fact, based on the fusion of a baritone's full, burnished timbre with a tenor's smooth, silken finish, by turns brilliant and affecting. This enabled him to achieve inflections of melting sensuality, now in caressing and elegiac tones, then in outbursts of fiery, impetuous passion. The clarion brilliance of his high notes, the steadiness of the sound, his exceptional breath control and his impeccable intonation combined to form a unique vocal instrument. One of his most memorable roles was that of the Duke of Mantua in Verdi's *Rigoletto*. But the legend of Caruso, considered the greatest tenor of the century, was due to a temperament as warm and vehement as his voice.

GIOVANNI MARTINELLI

(Born in Montagnana, October 22, 1885; died in New York, February 2, 1969)

As a boy, this Italian tenor sang and played the clarinet. He made his debut in Milano at the Teatro dal Verme in Rossini's *Stabat*

135

Mater. His Metropolitan debut in *La Bohème* on November 20, 1913, initiated a New York career that lasted without interruption for thirty years. Martinelli sang with the company in nearly 1,000 performances of thirty-six operas. The clarion ring of his upper register, the distinctness and purity of his declamation, and the sustained legato phrasing made possible by remarkable breath control were the outstanding features of his mature style. Martinelli retained his vocal powers to an advanced age, singing his last Othello in Philadelphia in 1947. His final appearance was in Seattle at the age of eighty-two.

JUSSI BJORLING
(Born in Stora Tuna, Sweden, February 5, 1911; died in Stockholm, September 9, 1960)

A Swedish tenor, Bjorling was first taught by his father. Starting in 1916 he made many concert tours with his father and two brothers. In 1928 he entered the Stockholm Conservatory, where he studied with Joseph Hislop and John Forsell. He made his recognized debut at the Royal Swedish Opera on August 20, 1930, as Don Ottavio in *Don Giovanni.* His repertory was mostly Italian. American audiences were especially delighted by the refined art of the Swedish tenor. His voice was a true tenor of velvety smoothness, though capable of ringing high notes of considerable power. Admirably schooled, he showed remarkable consistency from the top to the bottom of his register throughout his thirty-year career. One of his best roles was a Rodolfo in Puccini's *La Bohème.*

NICOLAI GEDDA
(Born in Stockholm, July 11, 1925)

A Swedish tenor with a Russian father and Swedish mother. As a boy he trained in Leipzig, where his father was the choirmaster at the Russian Orthodox church in 1924. On April 8, 19??, he made his debut at the Stockholm Opera as Chapelou in Adam's *Le Postillon de Longjumeau.* He was an instant success. Gedda has over 100 recordings of opera, operetta, oratorio, and lieder to his credit. A fine linguist, speaking and singing in seven languages, and with a large operatic and recital repertory, he commands the range of vocal and idiomatic style for Cellini and Pfitzner's *Palestrina,* Tchaikovsky's

Herman, and Fauré's songs. He is one of the most versatile and gifted of contemporary artists.

LUISA TETRAZZINI
(Born in Florence, June 29, 1891; died in Milano, April 28, 1940)

An Italian soprano, Tetrazzini had an unheralded Covent Garden debut on November 2, 1907, as Violetta in *La Traviata,* which caused a sensation. She possessed technical gifts of the highest order and could dazzle audiences with the ease and agility of her chromatic scales, both ascending and descending, and with her staccato, trills, and florid effects of every kind, especially above the staff. Around the high B-flat and C, where most Italian sopranos begin to thin out and become acid, her tonal emission remained as round and full as ever. Her tone was warm clarinet-like beauty. Her *cantilena* was shapely, spontaneous, and flowing. Between 1908 and 1914 were the years of her prime.

LUCIANO PAVAROTTI
(Born in Modena, October 12, 1935)

An Italian tenor, Pavarotti studied with Arrigo Pola and Ettore Campogalliani. He won the international competition at the Teatro Reggio Emilia in 1961 and made his debut there as Rodolfo in *La Bohème.* He made his debut at La Scala as the Duke of Mantua in 1965, and in 1967 sang there in Verdi's *Requiem* to mark the centenary of Toscanini's birth. He first appeared in the U.S. in 1968. He has a bright, incisive voice with a typically open, Italianate production, full and vibrant through its range, with penetrating high notes. His energy and musicianship are attractively combined.

Singing as a Spiritual Experience

We sing with the mind, through the body. Tone flows out from the tonal center of consciousness as vibration. It is carried on the surface of the will, sustained but never forced by the will power. The vocal cords transform mental tone into physical sound. The will still controls the tone, through the physical medium of the breath. Breath does not create tone, it merely floats the tone as the physical carrier of the transformed mental impulse. That's why singing is a spiritual experience, and not simply a physical technique. The rule is: Relax and sing, contract and bellow.

Italian Music Terms
A capella—without instrumental accompaniment.
Adagio—slowly (between andante and largo)
Allegretto—not too fast (between andante and allegro)
Allegro—Fast
Alto—Lower range female voice (also called contralto)
Andante—Moderate speed (between allegretto and adagio)
Aria—An elaborate composition for solo voice
Arpeggio—notes of a chord sung or played one after another
Crescendo—From soft to loud (opposite is decrescendo)
Forte—Loud
Tenor—the highest natural voice of a male
Soprano—The highest range for a female voice
Sostenuto—Sustaining the tone to or beyond its nominal value
Piano—Soft
Pianissimo—Very soft
Pianissimo forte—From soft to loud

Italian Kitchen Buzz-words

English	Italian
Almond	Mandorle
Artichoke	Carciofo
Basil	Basilico
Beans	Fagioli
Bread	Pane
Cheese	Formaggio (*or* caccio)
Chocolate	Cioccolata
Coffee	Caffè
Eggplant	Melanzane
Fennel	Finocchio
Lettuce	Lattuga
Marinade	Marinara
Mushrooms	Funghi
Olive oil	Olio di oliva
Oranges	Arance
Peppers	Peperoni
Pine Nuts	Pignoli
Rice	Riso
Sauce	Salsa
Soup	Zuppa (minestra)
Spinach	Spinacci
Sweets	La Dolce
Tomato	Pomodoro
Wine	Vino

A Trip to Italy

In this section I'd like to share with you a glimpse of Italy. For those who are planning to go to Italy or for those who are returning, I'm sure you'll enjoy the *informatione* that follows.

All Roads Lead to Rome

Italy is one of the oldest countries on the planet, a place where civilization has enjoyed a continuous history. It is also one of the newest, for it united under one government only in the 1860s. Italy is considered a country of art. But as you dig into its history, you find that it is also a country of law-makers, builders, and thinkers. Many of the great ideas that guide the world today were born in Italy.

On a spring morning of the year 753 B.C., Rome was founded by Romulus who, with his brother Remus (so the tale goes), had been abandoned as a child on the banks of the river Tiber, and suckled by a she-wolf. Even before this, the Etruscans, descendants of of Aeneas of Troy, had founded other towns on the Alban Hills. Three thousand years ago the history of Italy was already in full swing.

Romulus was the first of the "Seven Kings of Rome." A republic lasting over half a millennium was the first instance of an enduring democratic government in the world. The Roman Legions proved invincible in their many wars and the republic grew so that by the time Christ was born, the Roman Empire ruled the entire known world. As a universal empire, Rome continued for another four hundred years, establishing everywhere the principles of law by which we still live.

Seas of Blue-Green Splendor

Washed on three sides by the sea, Italy's total coastline measures some 5,310 miles. Rocky, wooded cliffs are indented by an infinite variety of beaches and bays. Along the full length of Liguria, Italy's

ITALY

northwest coastline, extend the two Italian rivieras, with Genoa in the middle. Further to the west, almost an extension of the French Côte d'Azur, is the Riviera di Ponente, including such famous seaside resorts as San Remo, Alassio, and Varazze. Just east of the Ponente lies the Riviera di Levante, boasting Nervi, Portofino, Santa Margherita, Rapallo, and Sestri Levanti.

Other beaches you should visit are: Forte dei Marmi, Viareggio, Castiglioncello, Porto Santo Stefano, Porto Ercole and the Island of Elba in Tuscany; Ostia (the Roman *lido* or "beach"), Fregene, Anzio, Netuno in Lazio; the islands of Capri and Ishia, Sorrento, Positano, Amalfi,and Maiori on the gulfs of Naples and Salerno; the sandy southern coastline of Calabria; Taormina, the Aeolian Islands and Mondello in Sicily, and the Emerald Coast of Sardinia.

Along northeastern Italy's Adriatic coast are Grado, the Venice and Jesolo *lidos*, and Lignano Sabbiadoro. Toward the south are the enchanting string of towns along the coast of Romagna, among which Milano Marittima (near Ravenna), Cervia, Rimini, Riccione, and Cattolica stand out. Further south are the sandy beaches of Pescara and Francavilla al Mare in the Marches and Abruzzi. On the coast of Apulia there is the *lido* of Siponto on the Gulf of Manfredonia, the Promontory of the Gargano, and the Tremiti Islands.

Skiing Anyone!

Italy is separated from France, Switzerland, Austria, and Yugoslavia by the Alps, the highest and the most fascinating mountains in Europe. Almost all of the southern Alpine slopes are in Italy. The highest peaks are Mont Blanc (14,782 feet), Monte Rosa (15,217 feet), the Matterhorn (14,780 feet), and the Gran Paradiso (13,324 feet). These giants are all found in the Val d'Aosta, an area that is not only unique but perhaps the most beautiful of the whole Alpine range. It is a magic realm for the traveler, studded with mountain climbing, and holiday and winter-sport centers. The Val d'Aosta is rich in magnificent natural scenery, poetic traditions, monuments, and castles.

Those Healing Waters!

The restorative powers of the mineral waters and mud baths that bubble from Italian springs—many of them of volcanic origin—

have been renowned since Roman times; the remains of Roman baths are still to be seen in a number of the watering places. The accent on rest and recreation has made many spas into fashionable resort centers, with excellent hotels, casinos, golf courses, and theaters. The best known spas are Acqui, St. Vincent, and Lurisia in Piedmont; San Pellegrino, Salice Terme, Bagni di Bormio, and Sirmione in Lombardy; Abano and Montegrotto in Venezia; Merano in the Alto Adige; Roncegno and Levico in Trentino; Salsomaggiore in Emilia; Montectini and Chianciano in Tuscany; Fiuggi, close to Rome; Agnano, Castellamare di Stabia, near Naples; Ischia Porto on the island of Ischia; and Sciacca in Sicily.

What's the best season to go to Italy? (I knew you were going to ask!)

All seasons are good for traveling in Italy. From the flowers of the Ligurian Riviera to the Alpine snows, from the golden wheatfields of Apulia to autumn sunsets in Rome, there is a never-ending succession of light and color as the sky and sea, the isles and volcanoes, the lakes and mountains offer an ever-changing spectacle.

The busiest touring season is from May to October, but spring and autumn are the choice times.

Here are the best regions for each season:

Spring comes early throughout Italy and it's ideal for holidays in Florence, the Gulf of Naples, the Sorrento Peninsula, the Lipari Islands, Sicily, and Rome.

Summer is great for the many beach resorts along the Ligurian and Adriatic rivieras, and the magnificent beaches on the Tyrrhenian, Adriatic and Ionian shores in Sardinia. At this time of year, travel stays in the mountains are great at the alpine resorts such as Ortisei, Cervinia, Cortina d'Ampezzo, and in the Apennines at Abetone (Tuscany), Roccarso (Abruzzi), Sila (Calabria), or Mt. Etna in sunny Sicily.

Autumn is a season that is particularly nice at Merano and Bressanone in the Dolomites, on the lakes of Lombardy, in Rome, Apulia, and on Italy's beautiful islands. Fall is the best time for visiting the spas.

Winter is the best for the winter sport season. The best centers can be found not only in the Alps but in other parts of Italy, such as the Apennines, on the Aspromonte in Calabria, and in Sicily. The climate is especially mild on the Ligurian and Neapolitan shores and in Sicily.

La Musica per-favore!!
Opera and Musical Festivals

Opera as we know it began in Italy in the sixteenth century. The first great name in operatic history was Monteverdi. The Italian operatic heritage has flourished ever since in the works of Rossini, Donizetti, Bellini, Puccini, and—the greatest of all—Verdi. The most famous opera house in the world is La Scala in Milan. Named for Regina della Scala, wife of a Milanese duke, La Scala opened in 1778 and is known worldwide for the technical perfection of its productions. The season at La Scala runs from December through May. Other distinguished opera houses are in Rome Opera (Nov.-June), the San Carlo Opera in Naples (Dec.-May), La Fenice in Venice (Nov.-June), the Regio in Turin (Nov.-June), the Comunales in Bologne and Genoa (Jan.-June), the Petruzzelli in Bari (Jan.-June), and La Massimo Bellini in Catania (Dec.-May).

Many places have summer outdoor opera festivals presented in classic settings: the Arena at Verona, the Baths of Caracalla (where the great PBS special on the three greatest tenors of our time was filmed) in Rome, the Steristerio Arena at Macerata, and the Rocca Brancaleone at Ravenna.

The Maggio Musicale Fiorentino is an outstanding festival of concerts, opera, ballet and drama held during May and June in Florence. In the tiny Umbrian town of Spoleto, the annual Festival of Two Worlds (founded by Gian Carlo Menotti) has won international fame for its presentations of opera, music, theater, art, and film in June and July. Martina Franca (Taranto) in the Puglia region plays host to the Opera Festival of the Atria Valley. Two opera festivals honoring composers are the Rossini and Puccini opera festivals in Torre del Lago during August. There is also the Summer Operetta Festival presented in Trieste during July and August.

The Main Course, or Feed Me and I'll Follow You Anywhere!

The main characteristic of Italian cooking is its healthy balance: basic ingredients are cooked simply and retain their original goodness and freshness. This simplicity is linked to such a variety of flavors and rich inventiveness in preparation that the gourmet is delighted. If you would like to sample all kinds of cooking you should go not only to the well-known restaurants that feature regional cuisine (Tuscany, Bologna, Emilia, Rome, Naples, etc.), but to the modest *trattorie,* which are more homelike and where they are proud to have you taste their specialties. You should dine at restaurants where, weather permitting, you can eat outdoors. The hours passed under a *pergola* or on a sunlit terrace bright with the colors of curtains and parasols, gazing out over a landscape of green and gold, can be some of the most beautiful romantic memories in Italy.

Here is a selection of the main regional specialties that you should sample:

Piedmont—Fonduta (cheese with eggs and truffles), Agnolotti
(stuffed pasta), and toffees, chocolates, and *marrons glâces.*
Lombardy—Risotto alla Milanese (rice with saffron), minestrone (a
substantial soup stock and vegetables), Osso Buco alla Milanese
(knuckle of veal cutlets), cheeses (robiola, gorgonzola, stracchino,
Bel Pese), Panettone (a cake with candied citrus peel).
Venice—Risi e Bisi (soup rice and peas), Polenta (a cornmeal dish),
Zuppa di Pesce (fish soup), scampi (prawns), Fegato alla
Veneziana (calfs liver with onions).

Liguria—Minestrone, Lasagne al Pesto (broad flat pasta with Genoese sauce, very aromatic with garlic and basil), Torta Pasqualina (Easter pie with a filling of spinach, artichokes, and cheese).

Emillia—Lasagne Verdi (made with spinach), Cappelletti ("little hats" pasta), Scaloppe alla Bolognese (scallops), salami, cheeses (Parmigiano reggiano).

Tuscany—Bistecca alla Fiorentina (huge T-bone steak grilled over aromatic charcoal), Arista (roast pork), Cacciucco (fish soup), Trigliealla Livormese (red mullet cooked with tomatoes and oil).

Lazio—Fettuccine, Gnocchi (tiny cylinders of cornmeal or mashed potato boiled and eaten with meat and tomato sauce), Abbacchio (suckling lamb), Porchetta (pork rosted on a spit), Carciofi alla Giudia (artichokes fried in olive oil).

Campania—Spaghettialle Vongole (pasta with tomatoes and clams), scampi, triglie (mullet), and seppie (cuttlefish); the celebrated pizzas; cheeses (mozzarella, provola, caciocavallo).

Sicily—Caponata di Melanzane (eggplant), Pasta con le Sarde (pasta and sardines), splended fresh fruit—oranges, tangerines, grapefruit, grapes—and world-famous pastries such as Cannoli alla Siciliana, Cassata amd Pasta di Mandorie.

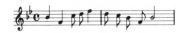

For the Wine Connoisseur, Ah Salute!

Wine is considered a food by gourmets and gourmands the world over. You will find many different varieties and tastes that complement any Italian meal, and some are even used in the preparation and cooking. Here is a list of some of the most famous regions and their special vinos.

Piedmont—Barolo, Barbara, Barbaresco, Freisa, Asti Spumante.
Lombardy—Frecciarossa, the rose wines of Lago di Garda.
Venice—Santa Maddalena, Santa Giustina, Termeno, Reisling,
    Teriano (all from the Trentino area), and Soave and Valpolicella
    from the Verona region.
Emilia—Lambrusco, Sangiovese.
Tuscany—Chianti, Brunello
The Marches—Verdiccio
Umbria—White Orvieto
Lazio—Wines of Castelli Romani, and the wine that is intrigingly
    named EST! EST! EST!
Abruzzo—Montepulciano
Campania—Gragnano, white Capri, Malvasia.
Calabria—Ciro, white Greco di Gerace.
Basilicata—Aglianico del Vulture
Sicily—Etna wines: Moscato from Pantelleria, Corvo di Salaparuta.
Sardinia—Vernaccia, Ogliastra, Oliena.

Some other Italian drinks include apéritifs blended principally over a base of the world-famous Piedmont vermouth, dessert wines (such as Marsala and Malvasia from Sicily), and sparkling wines from Piedmont, Venice, Tuscany, and the islands. Italy has good beers and a great variety of effervescent mineral waters.

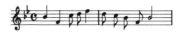

Olive Oils, What You Should Know About Them!

I would like to thank Craig Makela, president of the Santa Barbara Olive company (sixth generation), for giving me the scoop on what sometimes proves to be a somewhat confusing dilemma: Which type of olive oil should one cook with and how best to use this ever growing popular oil?

First let's classify the types of olive oils:

EXTRA VIRGIN—This oil has less than 1 percent oleic acidity and is considered perfect in flavor and aroma. The process is *sinolea*, cold-pressed, and the flavor tends to be delicate and peppery. The color is golden green and the aroma is fruity and fresh.

VIRGIN—This oil has an oleic acidity level between 1 and 5 percent and has a sharper taste. This is also cold-pressed (over-ripe olives that produce more oil), and the flavor is heavy and strong. The color runs from green to black, and the aroma is not the greatest.

PURE—This consists of a mixture of refined (chemically treated) olive oil and 5 to 10 percent olive oil. The process blends 10 percent virgin and 90 percent refined oil. The flavor is light, and the color is light green. The aroma is poor in most cases.

POMACE—This olive oil is chemically extracted from the pulp (pits) and or residue of the olives. The process is chemical, using a solvent extraction. The flavor is almost nonexistent, and the color runs from white to yellow. This oil has a poor aroma.

The main difference between first-class, extra-virgin olive oil and virgin olive oil is that the extra-virgin has 1 percent oleic acid and the virgin olive oil has from 1 percent to 5 percent oleic acid.

To test if you have genuine extra-virgin olive oil or chemically processed oil, place a small bottle of olive oil in the refrigerator for about four days. The chemically processed olive oil will turn white

149

and mass into a solid; the genuine extra-virgin oil will maintain the golden green color, and will create small granules of fat suspended in the liquid oil.

So what about cooking with these different kinds of olive oil? It seems that the best advice would be to cook with pure olive oil and season the dishes after cooking with the extra-virgin. If you cook with the extra-virgin, especially delicate dishes, the oil will overpower the other tastes. The nouveau cuisine chefs flavor food with extra-virgin olive oil. An example would be on a Caesar Salad—use pure olive oil so that you will be able to pick up the taste of the anchovies and capers and olives. Fish and pasta dishes should follow this rule of thumb, too.

Let's Talk Olives

All olive oil is cold-pressed. This is the first step after picking the olives for processing. The color will be in direct relation to the variety of olive. There are three main stages of color: green, red, and black. It's really a matter of the olive grower's preference as to what type he or she likes to use to produce a good olive oil. Some feel that the best olives for processing are those that are allowed to ripen on the tree.

There are about four ways to cure olives:

1. The Spanish cure involves a lye process
2. The Sicilian cure involves water and salt
3. The Greeks use a dry salt-cure
4. Pure water cure

These cures pull out the glycoside from the olive; glycoside is the unpalatable, indigestible substance in the olive.

The red ripe olive has a sweet, fruity flavor; the green olive has a pungent, strong, and bitterly stringent taste; and the black olive has an "old" taste. There are over sixty varieties of olives worldwide. It takes about five years from shoot to fruit, and between seven and eight years for a good commercial crop to grow.

It takes about two hundred medium-size olives to make 5 ounces of extra-virgin olive oil. The olive itself is about 50 percent water, 22 percent oil, 19.1 percent sugar, 1.6 percent protein, and

7.3 percent other organic substances. Olives are not fattening—they average 4 to 5 calories each and *contain no cholesterol.* Olives naturally contain vitamins B-6, B-12, A, and C, as well as fiber, ash, protein, and most of the essential minerals needed for a healthy diet.

Some olive folk lore: "A branch over the door keeps out witches and wizards."

Here is a recipes for home-cured olives that I would like to share with you.

WATER -CURED OLIVES

Take 2.5 gallons of fresh, crunchy green olives. Crack each olive with a stone. Place them in a 5-gallon plastic container and cover completely with water. Place a plate and with a rock on top of them over the olives—otherwise the olives will float above the water. Change the water every day. (Don't feel too guilty if you miss a day here or there). After three or four weeks, taste the olives to see if all the bitterness has leached out. Dry the olives overnight, spread out on the top of a table, then put them in a big mixing bowl.

Chop two big bunches of mint. Peel and finely chop two heads of garlic. Mix this into the olives. Add 3 cups of extra-virgin olive oil, 1 cup of good wine vinegar, and salt to taste. Leave the olives in the bowl and stir them into jars and cover them thoroughly with olive oil. Store these olives in the refrigerator, but serve at room temperature. They should be eaten within two months.

—ANGELO GARRO

ITALIAN GOVERNMENT TRAVEL OFFICE
MAIN OFFICE IN ROME, ENTE NAZIONALE
ITALIANO PER IL TURISMO-ENIT.

Via Marghera, 2-00185, Rome, Italy
Tel: (06) 49711 Telefax: 4463379

ITALIAN GOVERNMENT TRAVEL OFFICE
IN U.S. AND CANADA

500 North Michigan Avenue, Chicago, Illinois 60611
Tel: (312) 644-0990 TLX: 0255160 Telefax: 644-3019

1 Place Ville Marie, Suite 1914, Montreal, Quebec H3B 3m9
Tel: (514) 866-7667 TLX: 0021-525607 Telefax: 392-1429

630 Fifth Avenue, New York, New York 10011
Tel: (212) 245-4822 TLX: 236024 Telefax 586-9249

360 Post Street, San Francisco, California 94108
Tel: (415) 392-6206 TLX: 067623 Telefax: 392-6852

Measurement Conversions

U.S. System to Metric

Tsp.	Tbl.	Cup	Oz.	Lb.	Met. grams
pinch (less than 1/8 tsp.)					0.5 gr.
dash (3 drops to 1/4 tsp.)					1.25 gr.
1 tsp.					5.0 gr.
3 tsp.	1 tbl.		1/2 oz.		14.3 gr.
	2 tbl.		10 oz.		28.35 gr.
	4 tbl.	1/4 cup	2 oz.		56.7 gr.
	8 tbl.	1/2 cup	4 oz.		113.4 gr.
	16 tbl.	1 cup	8 oz.	1/2 lb.	226.8 gr.
	32 tbl.	2 cups	16. oz.	1 lb.	453.6 gr.
	64 tbl.	4 cups	32. oz.	1 lb.	907. gr. (0.45 kg)

Temperature Conversions

Farenheith		*Centigrade*
-10°	=	-23.3° (freezer storage)
0°	=	-17.7°
32°	=	0° (water freezes)
50°	=	10°
68°	=	20° (room temp.)
100°	=	37.7°
150°	=	65.5°
205°	=	96.1° (water simmers)
212°	=	100° (water boils)
300°	=	148.8°
325°	=	162.8°
350°	=	177.0° (baking temp.)
375°	=	190.5°
400°	=	204.4° (hot oven)
425°	=	218.3°
450°	=	232° (very hot oven)
475°	=	246.1°
500°	=	260.0° (boil)

Index of Recipes

155

Specialità

La Dolce Vita

Sing and Cook Books

These are a series of books about the joy of *Singing and Cooking* in the Romance languages—Italian, French, and Spanish. Food and song, love and romance—they go very well together.

These books capture the part of each culture that is so universal in its nature that almost everyone can relate to the content. The melodies, the mood, and the atmosphere all lend themselves to the best recipes from each ethnic kitchen.

Sing and Cook Italian takes one on a journey through Italy, especially southern Italy, where pasta is abundant and the sea provides the fresh fish for many of the dishes. The songs and melodies from the classic folk songs of Italy will entice one into the mood of the beautiful Italian culture in their own kitchen.

Sing and Cook French allows one to experience the beautiful countryside of France and to revel in its delicious country dishes. It takes one to the most famous city, Paris, and creates the music of the great French singers. You will feel like Edith Piaf and Jacques Brel as you sing those haunting melodies that come straight from the heart.

Sing and Cook Spanish brings into your kitchen the warm colors and spices of this exciting culture. With every blend of seasoning you will be able to recreate this lush culture right in your own kitchen. The mood will almost certainly make you sing and dance like a toreador in full costume and your dinners will make everyone shout *Ole!*

These books are meant to be used and not just to sit on one's shelf. They will be filled with not only great recipes, but also great teaching aids to singing in Italian, French, and Spanish. They are timely and will be a great gift for just about anyone!

The books come with an audio tape to enable people to sing along with Andy Lo Russo while cooking.

FORTHCOMING BOOKS:

Sing & Cook French

Sing & Cook Spanish

TO ORDER...

✉ **POSTAL ORDERS:**
Send to:
Sing & Cook
P.O. Box 91725
Santa Barbara, California 93190
• $19.95 plus $3.95 to cover shipping and handling. For shipments to California, add 7.75% state sales tax.

Other items by Andy Lo Russo (allow 4-6 weeks delivery):

• **The Original PolkAerobics Video Program** ($19.95+$3.50S&H)
A low-impact way to exercise, done with a partner, and to the time of a polka beat. Beginning, intermediate, and advanced levels all on one video. (117 minutes—as seen on television)

• **The Pierogie Diet Book—
101 Fun Ways How to Use & Enjoy Pierogie** ($2.95+$1.00S&H)
A small booklet on the joys of making and using this delicious Eastern European pasta pocket. Done in a humorous way with rhymes you'll chuckle at all the way. Some traditional recipes included.
ISBN 0-962202-0-2

• **Sing & Cook Italian Logo Aprons**
Red, $13.95 + $2.95 shipping and handling.

Name _____

Address _____

City/State/Zip _____

Phone (with area code) _____

Please ship me ____ copies of *Sing & Cook Italian* at $19.95 per book (plus $3.95 S&H; California residents add 7.75% state sales tax).
I enclose a check/money order in the amount of: $_____.